WILDWOOD

MARIE WALLIN

CONTENTS

08 **Designs**
11 handknit designs by Marie Wallin

64 **Gallery**

66 **Patterns**

98 **Beacon Hill Country Park**

100 **British Breeds**

104 **Steeking**

108 **Information**

110 **Credits**

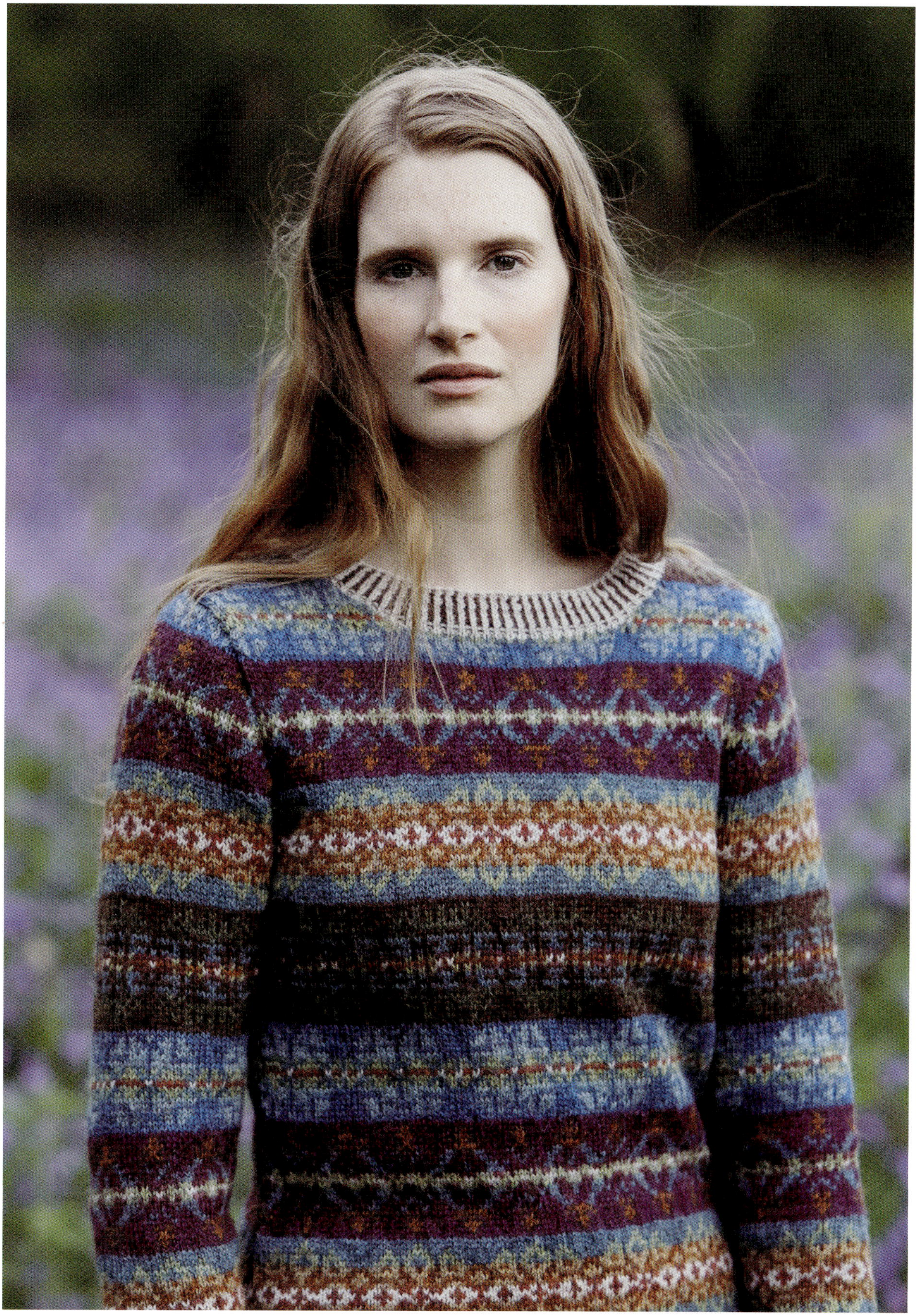

FOREWORD

WILDWOOD is a collection of eleven beautiful Fair Isle and stitch designs using my new yarn, BRITISH BREEDS.

Just over two years in developing, my BRITISH BREEDS yarn is the culmination of my knowledge of yarn and colour gained over a thirty two year career in knitwear design. This very special blend of wool from four different British sheep breeds is worsted spun combining all my passion and support for British Wool and British yarn spinning and production. You can read all about my venture to develop BRITISH BREEDS in a feature at the end of the book.

Photographed at Beacon Hill Country Park in rural Leicestershire, WILDWOOD is a collection of modern Fair Isle design with a hint of stitch texture. The twelve colours of BRITISH BREEDS have been specifically designed to work together beautifully in patterned colour work but also each individual shade works equally well as a stand alone single colour for solid colour knitting.

I hope that you are as enchanted by my new collection and my new yarn as much as myself. To be able to introduce my first collection featuring my own yarn is a very proud and special time in my life of knitting and design.

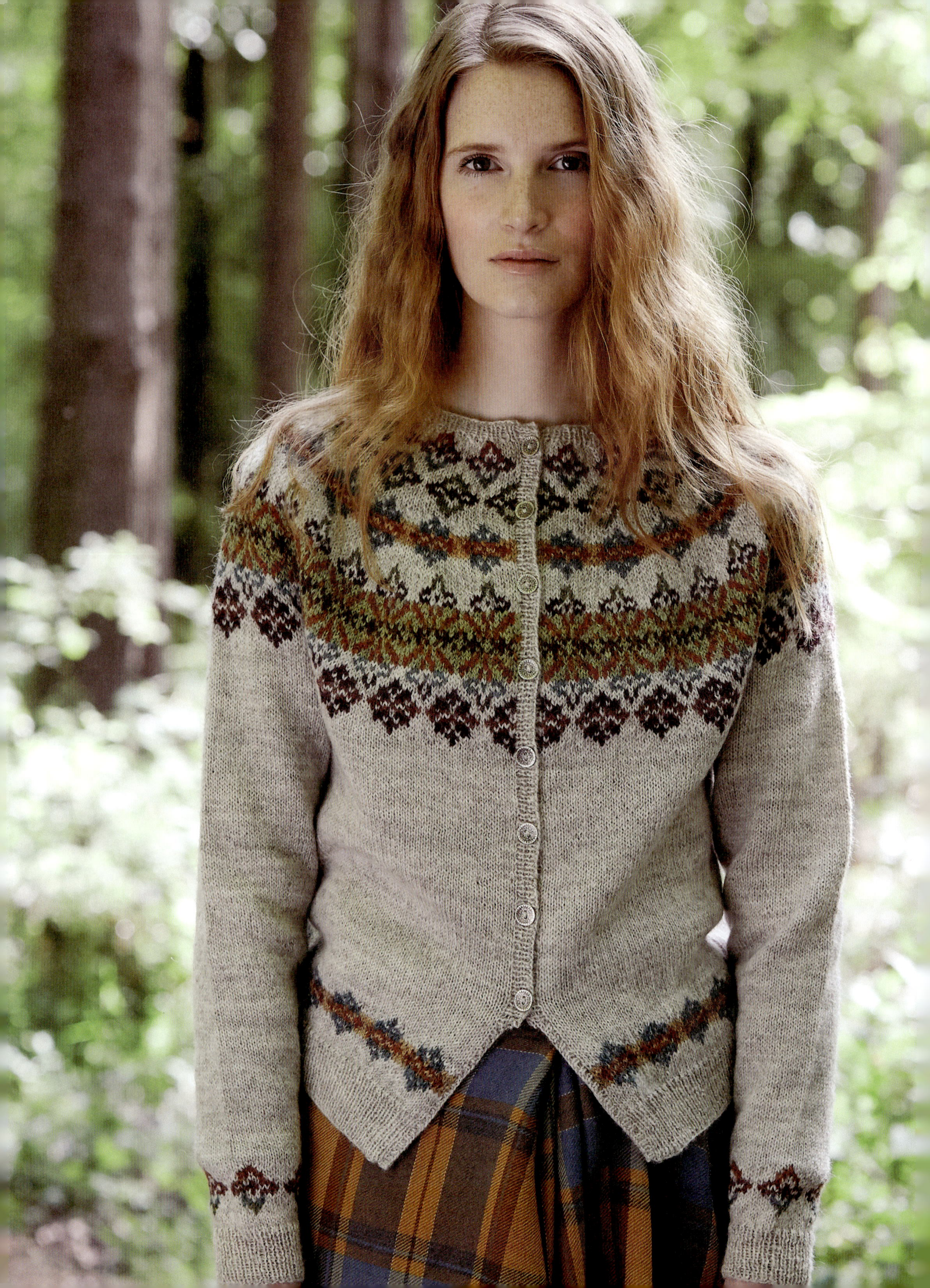

HAWTHORN

... is a beautiful Fair Isle yoke cardigan, knitted in the round and steeked. Using ten colours of BRITISH BREEDS, this Fair Isle design is inspired by Eastern European ornamental folk design.

WILDWOOD

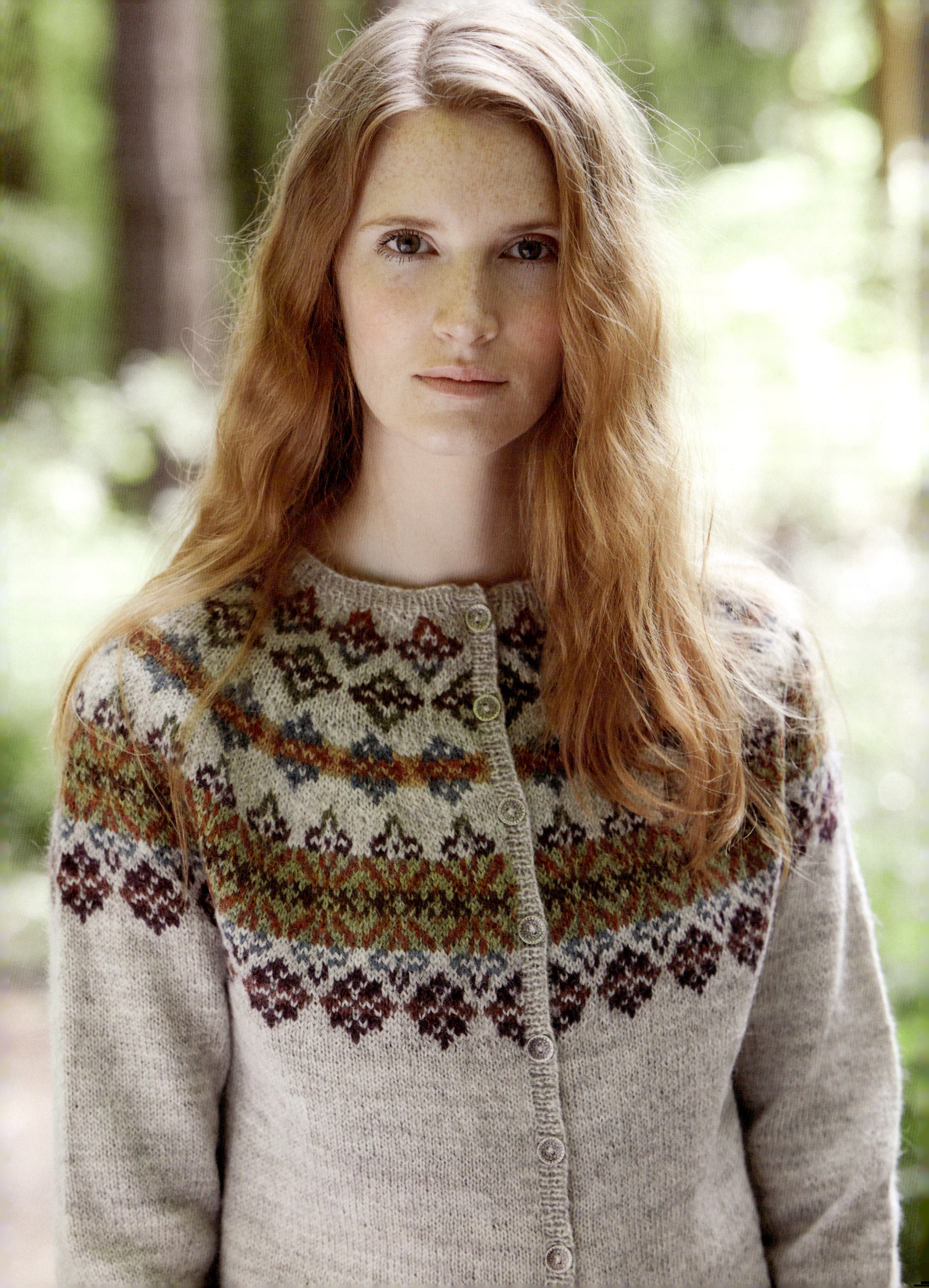

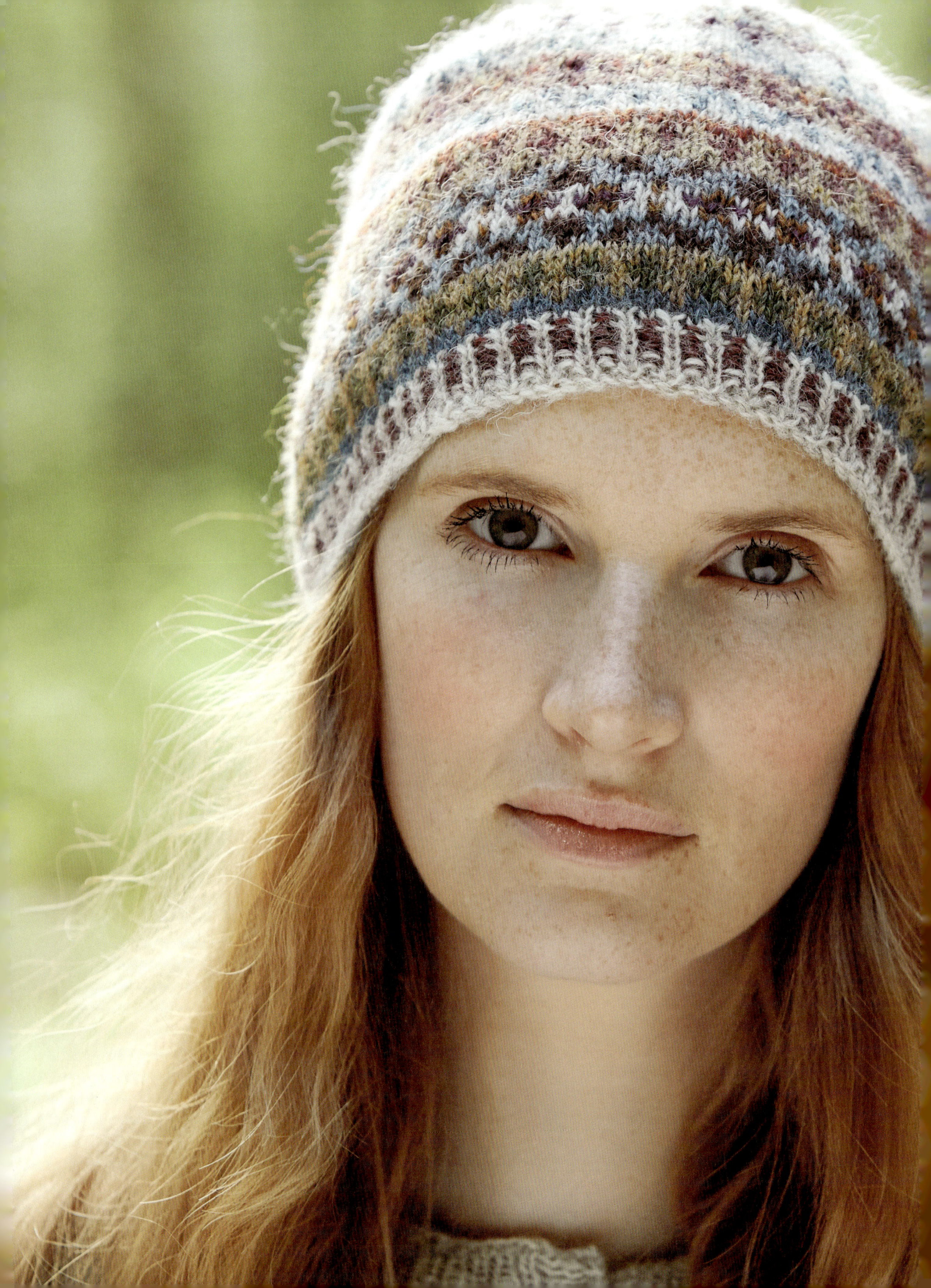

WALNUT TAM

This is a simple traditional Fair Isle tam knitted in the round and perfect to wear on chilly autumn days.

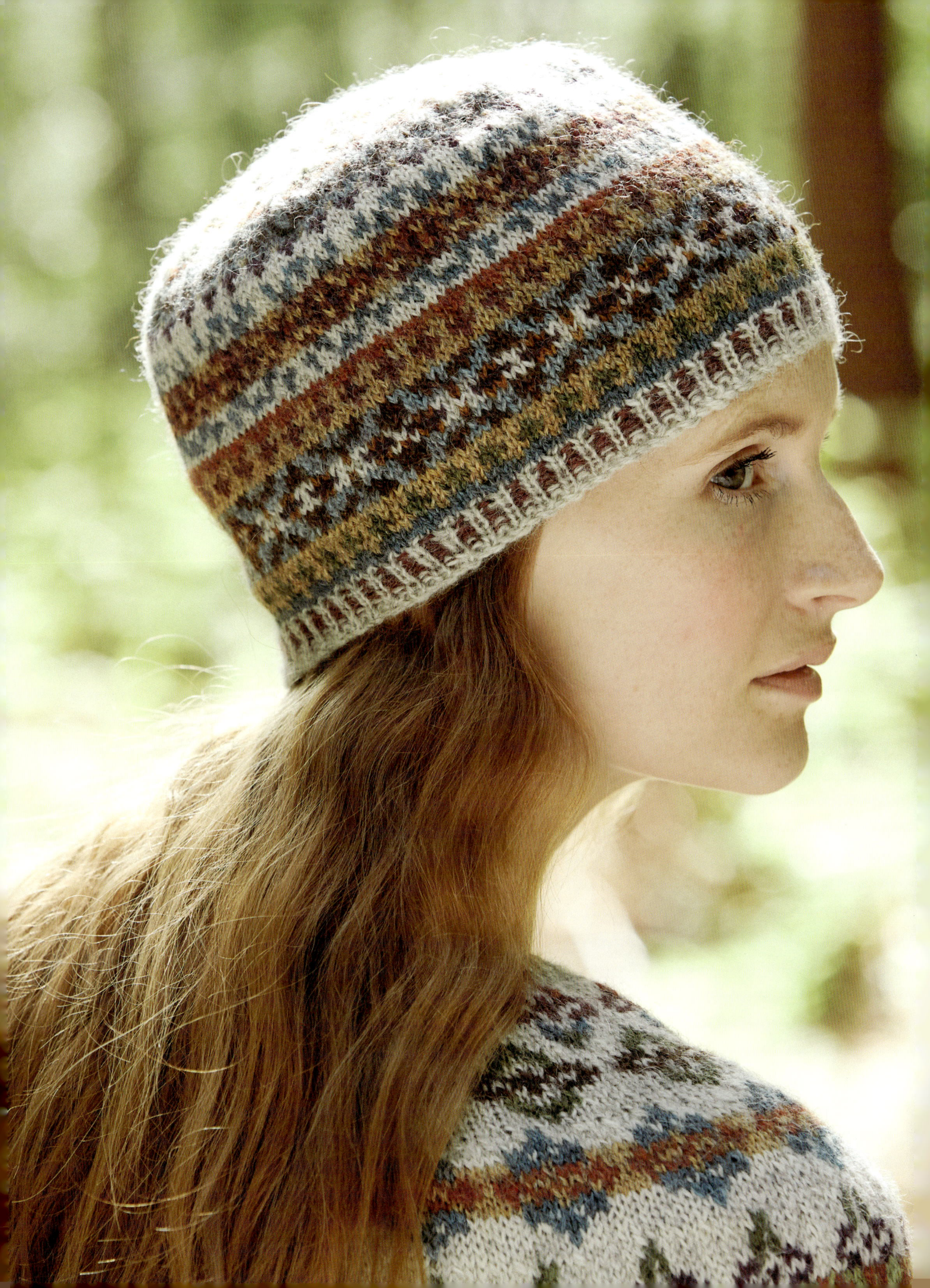

WILDWOOD

HOLLY

This understated modern Fair Isle design is inspired by the floral patterning found in antique Eastern European textiles. The simple top is semi-fitted and is intended to be worn as a layer piece.

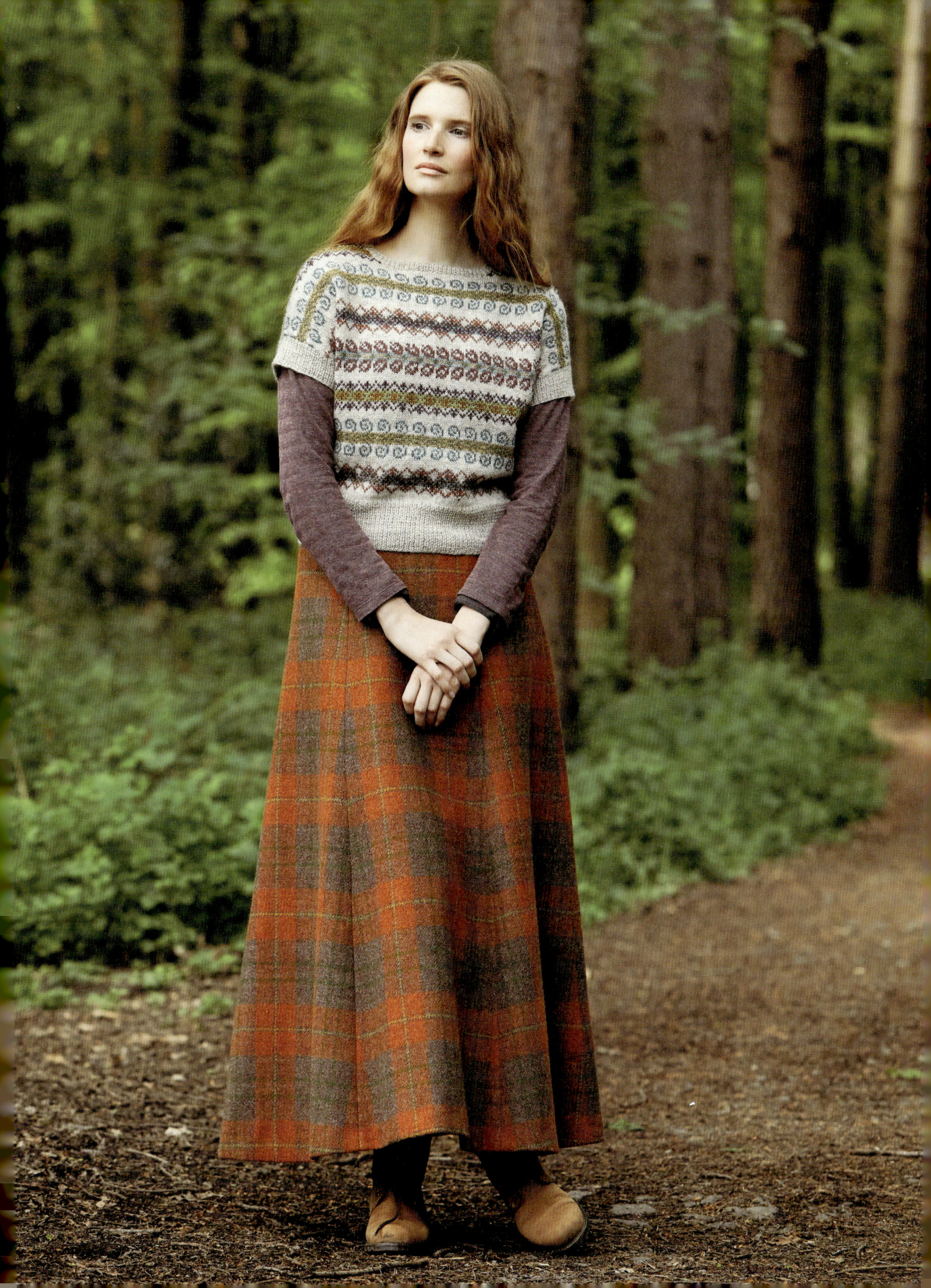

WILDWOOD

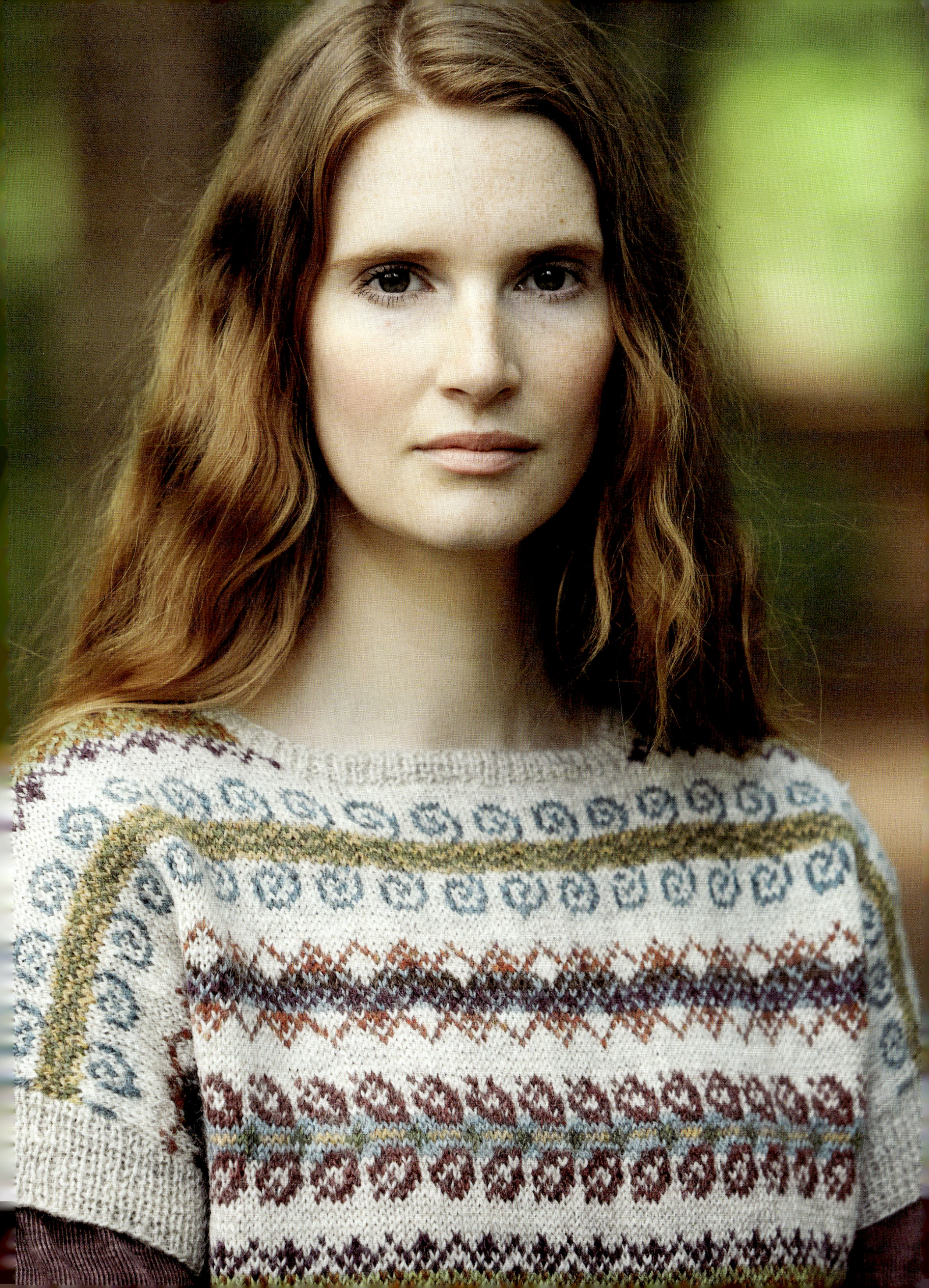

WILDWOOD

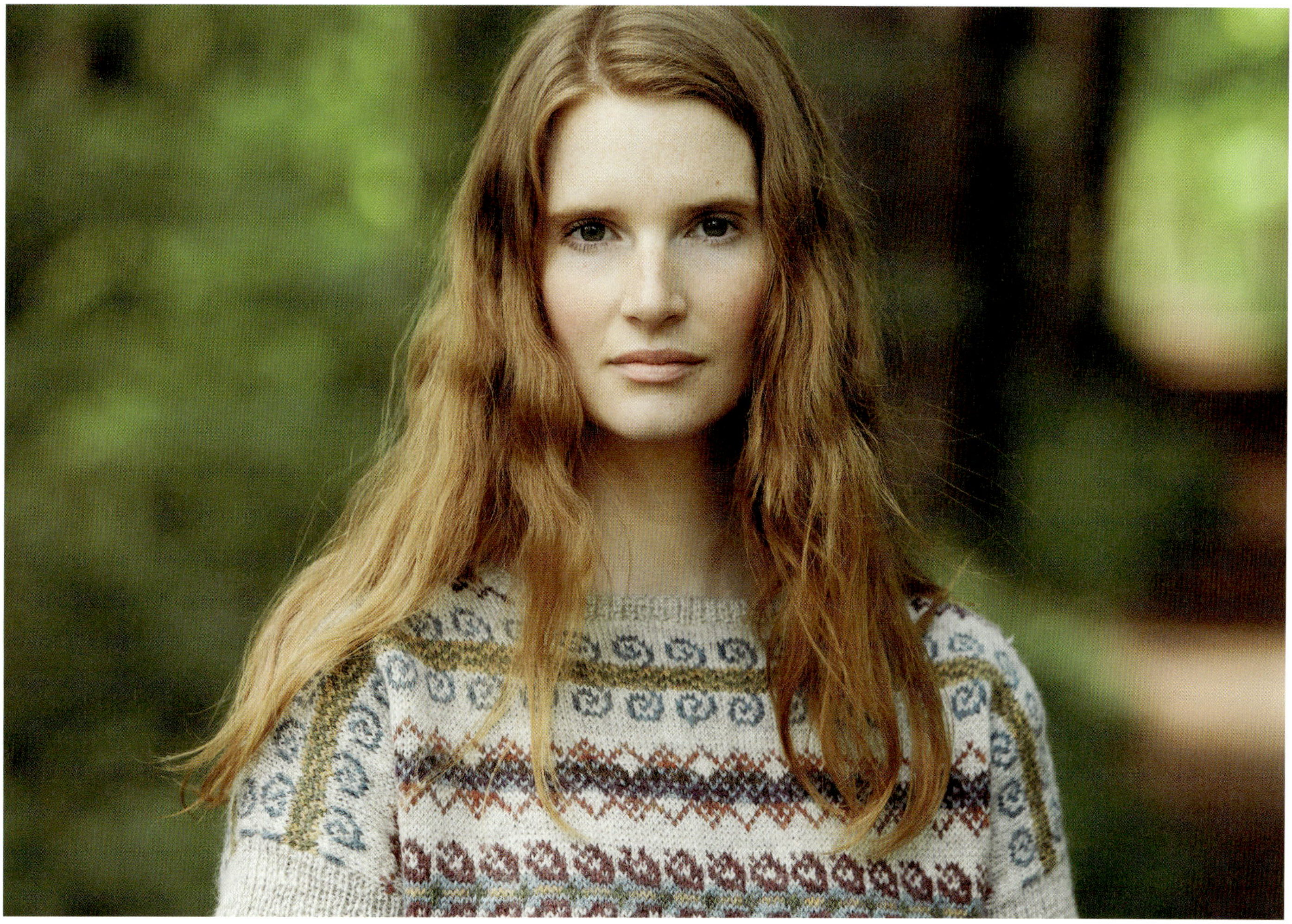

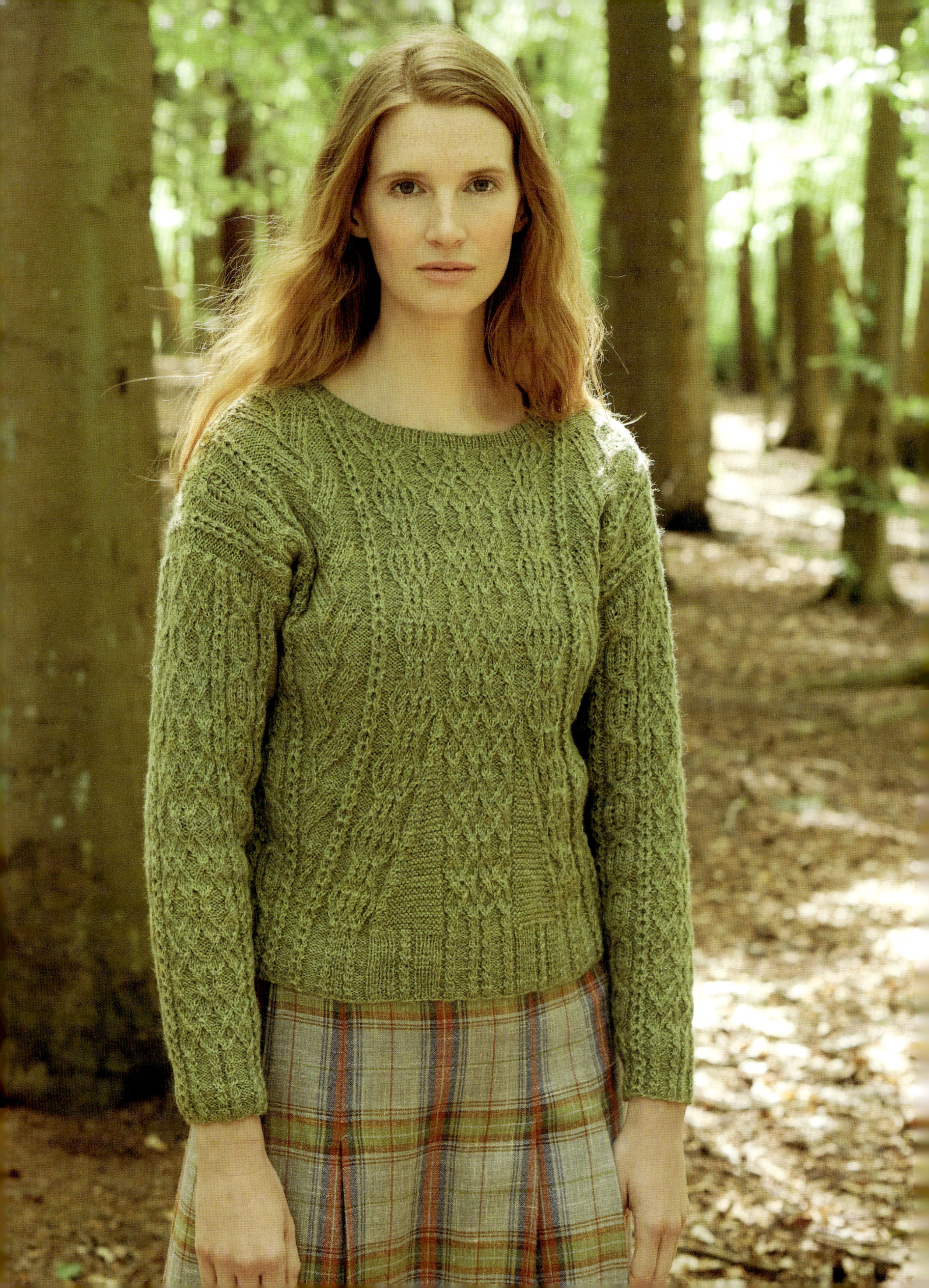

YEW

This is an all over stitch textured design using twisted stitches. The integral pattern shaping at the bottom of the sweater helps to turn this traditionally inspired design into a modern classic.

WILDWOOD

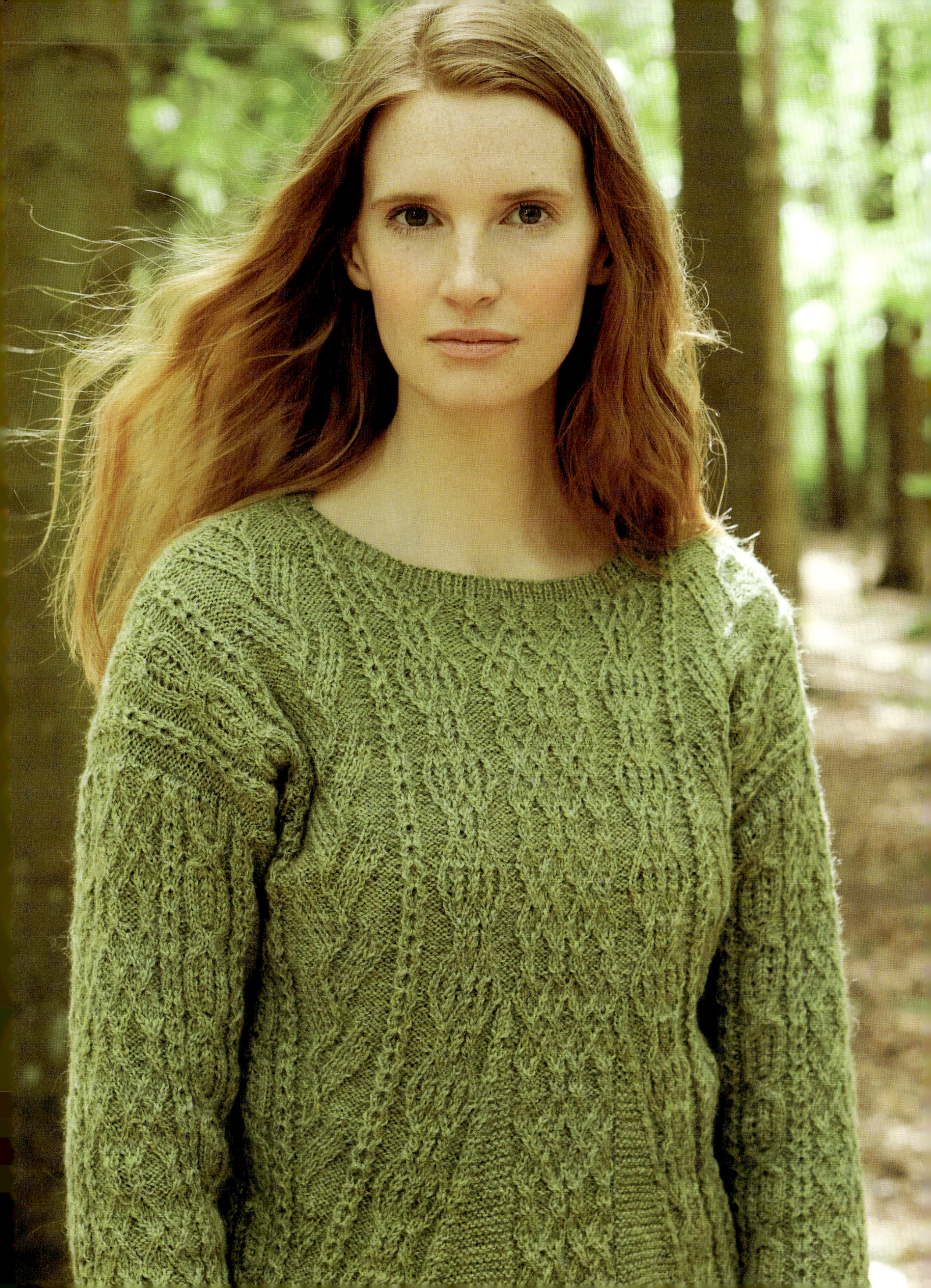

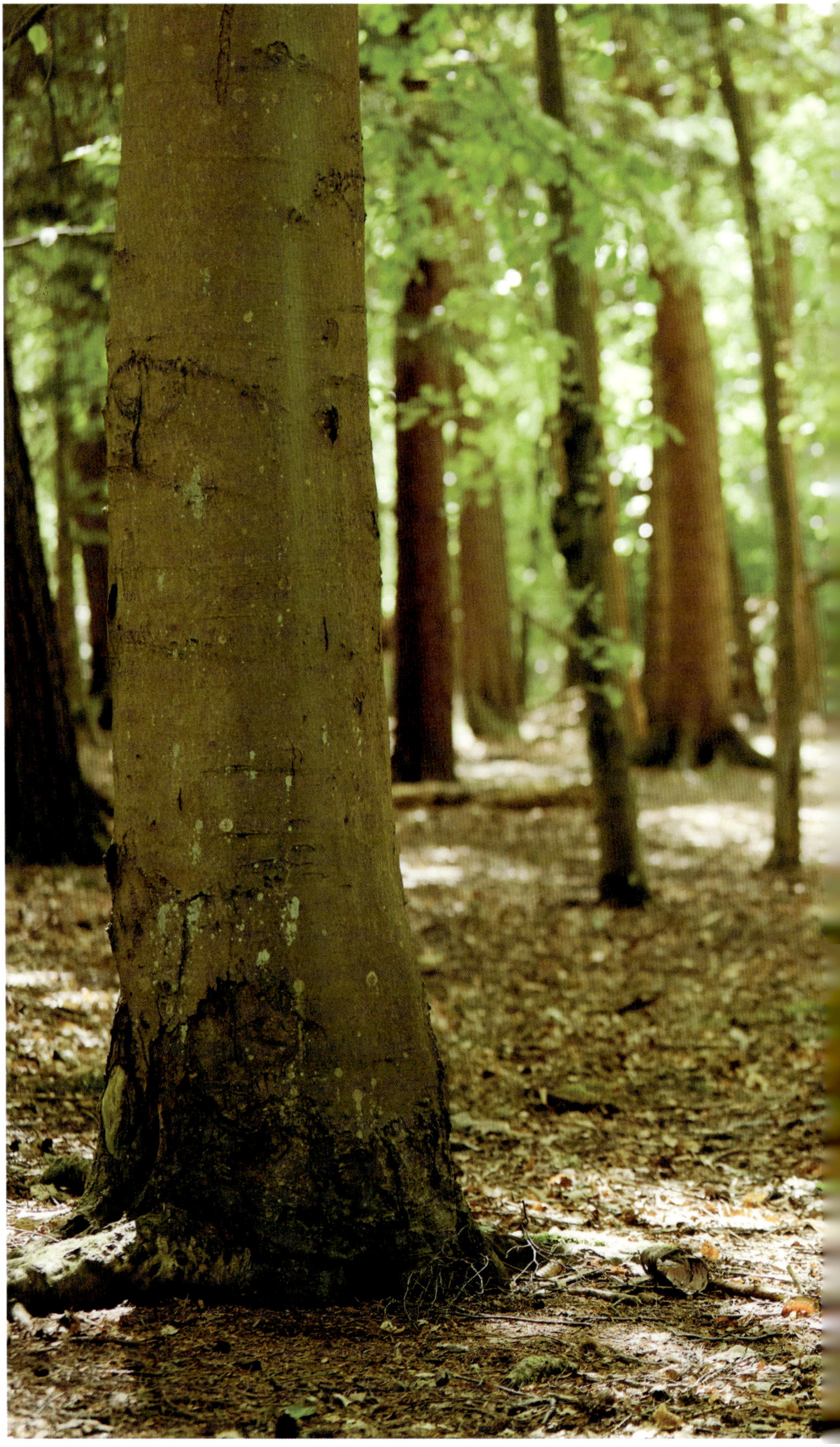

WILDWOOD

ROWAN COWL

...is a beautiful floral inspired cowl. This simple patterned design is essentially a single motif repeated throughout on a striping background of colour.

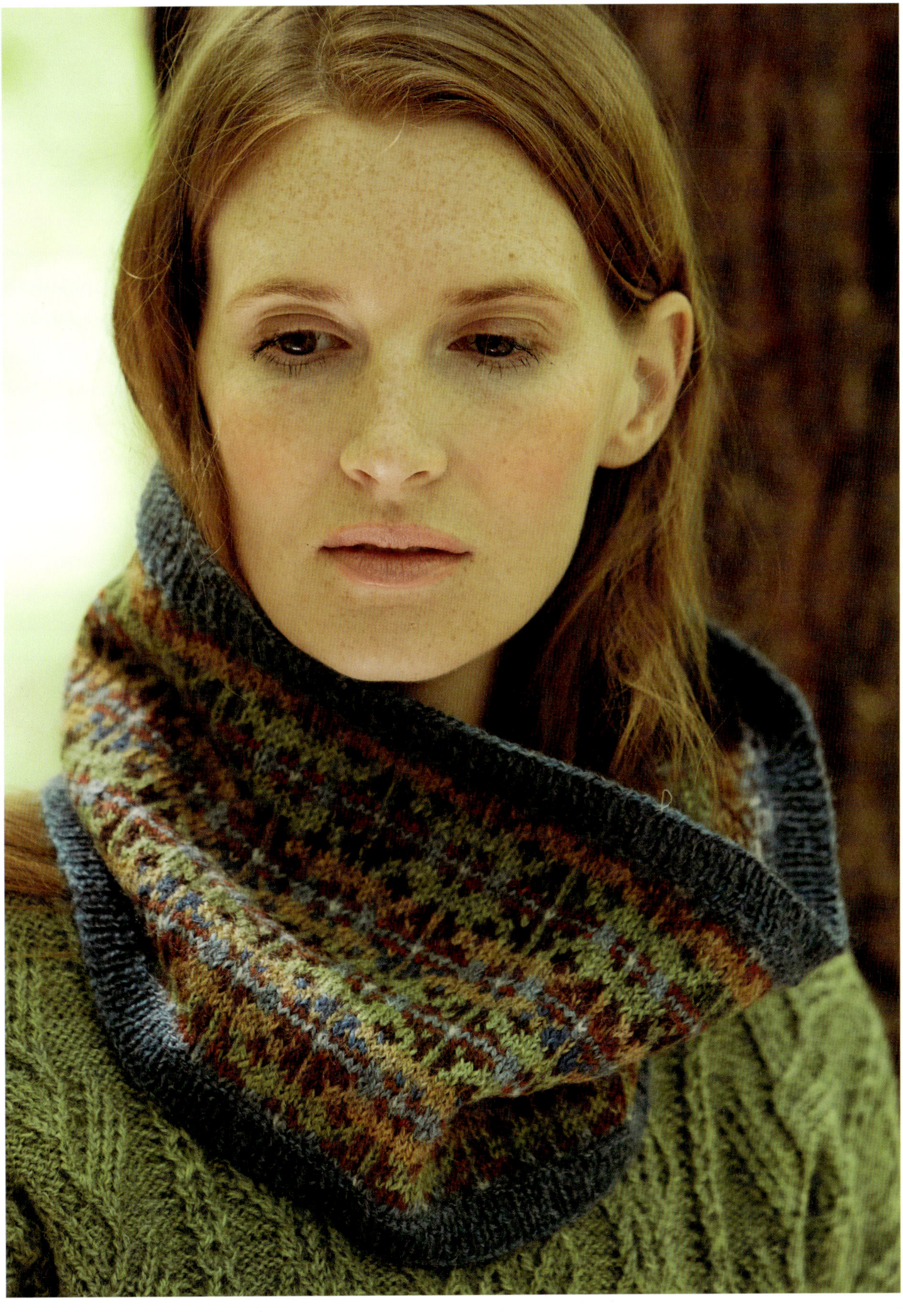

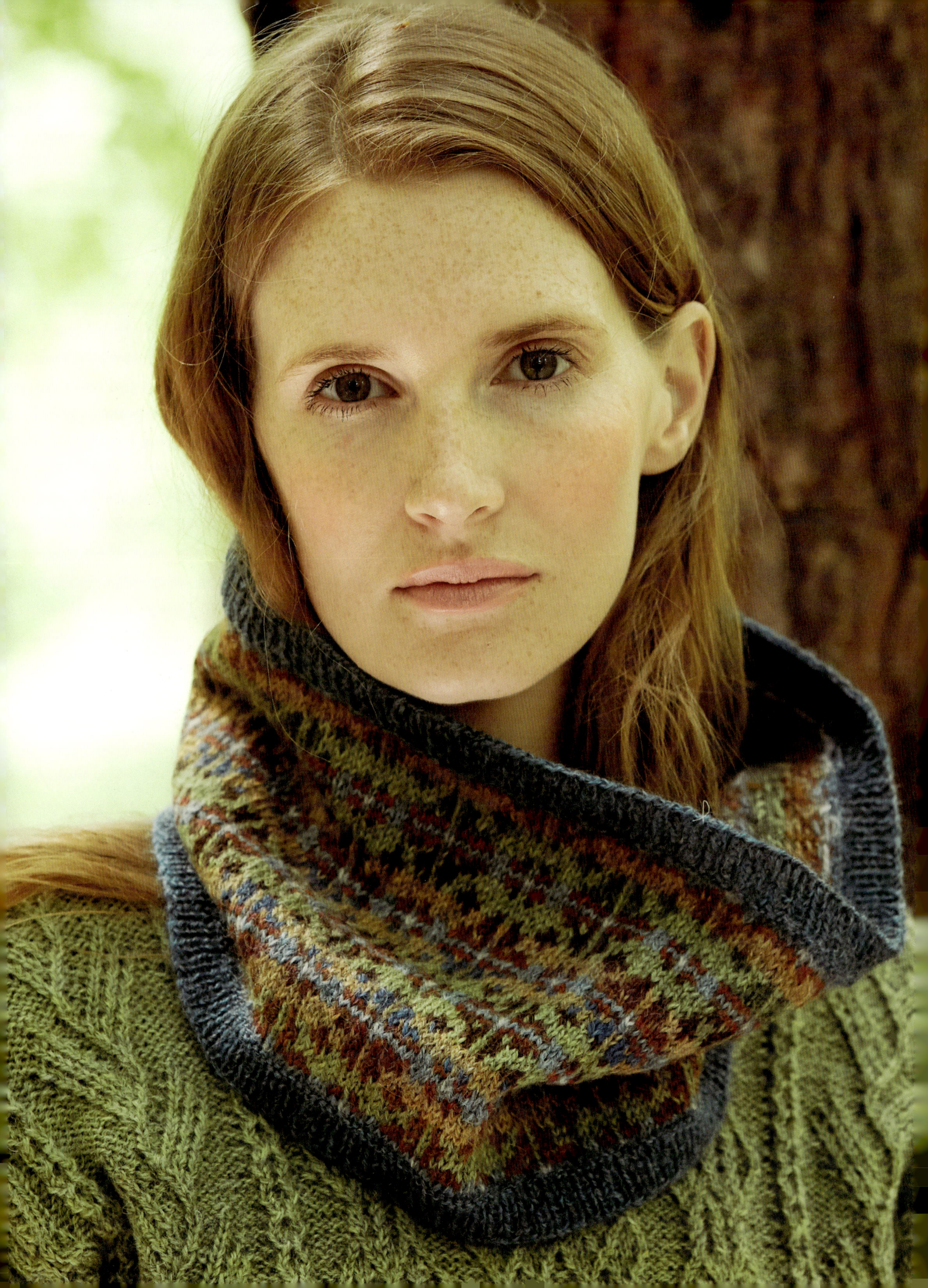

WILDWOOD

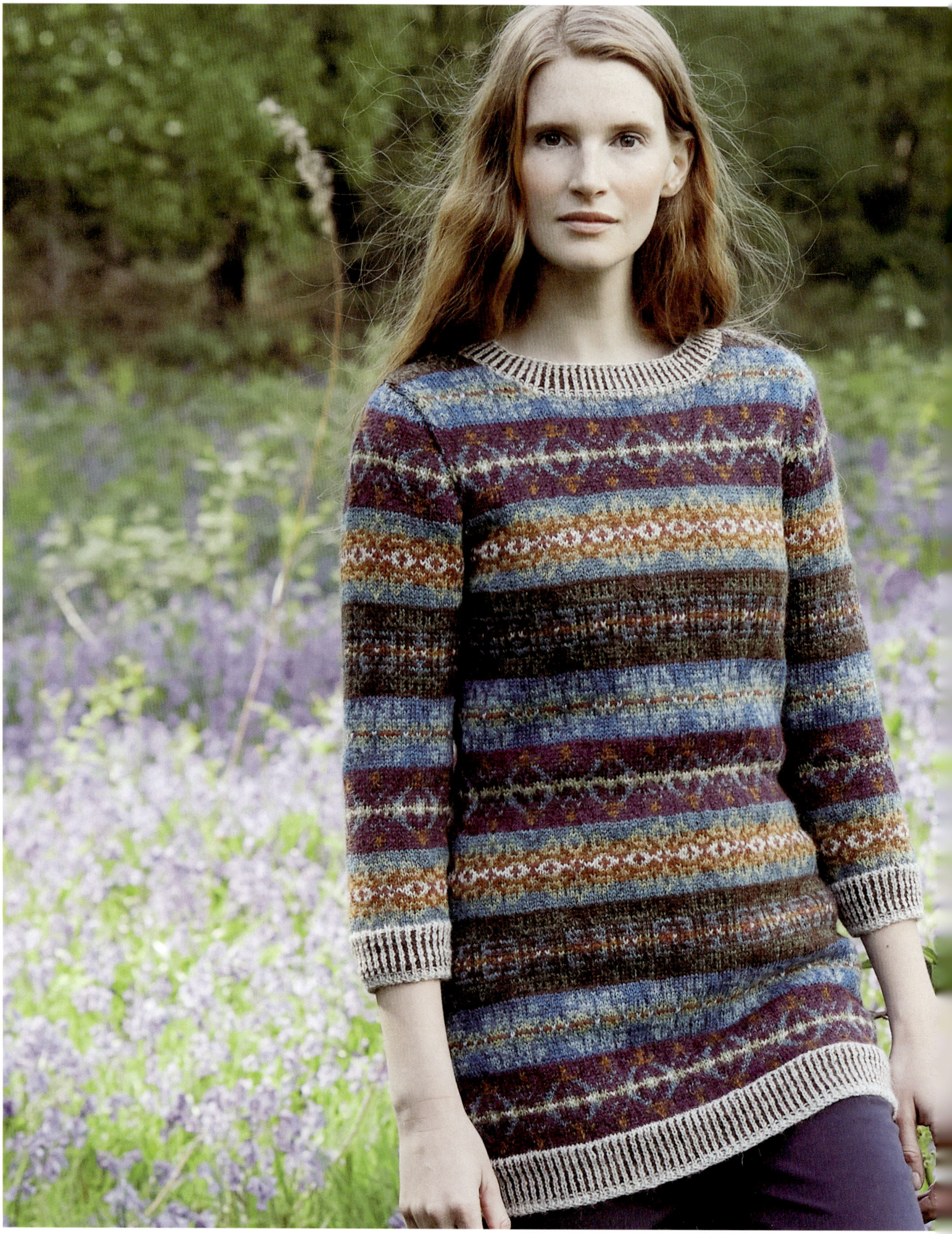

WILD ROSE

Probably my favourite design in the collection, WILD ROSE is a beautiful fitted tunic with three quarter length sleeves, and is intended to be worn as a layer piece. Using all twelve colours of BRITISH BREEDS this design is inspired by traditional Fair Isle motifs and patterning.

WILDWOOD

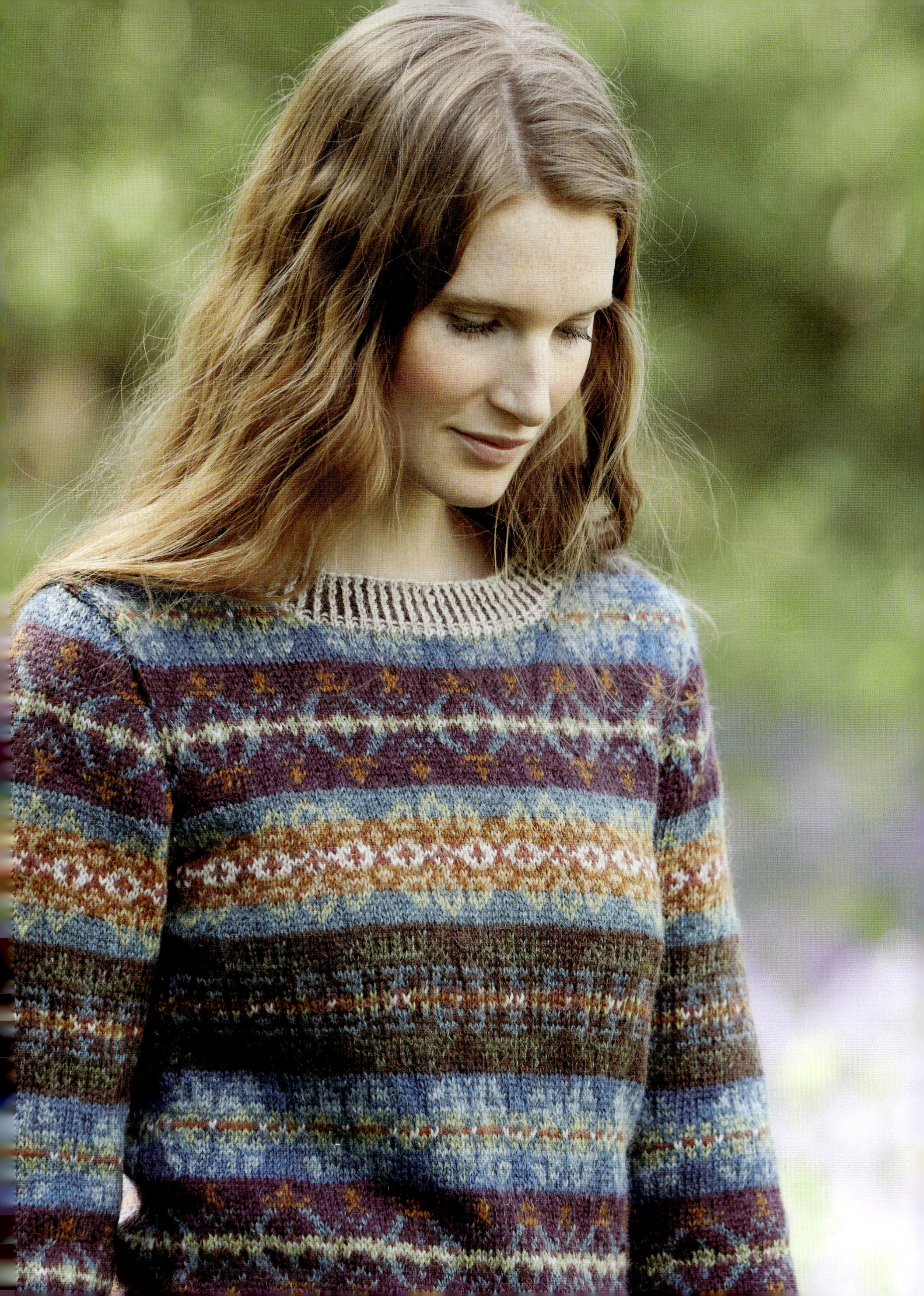

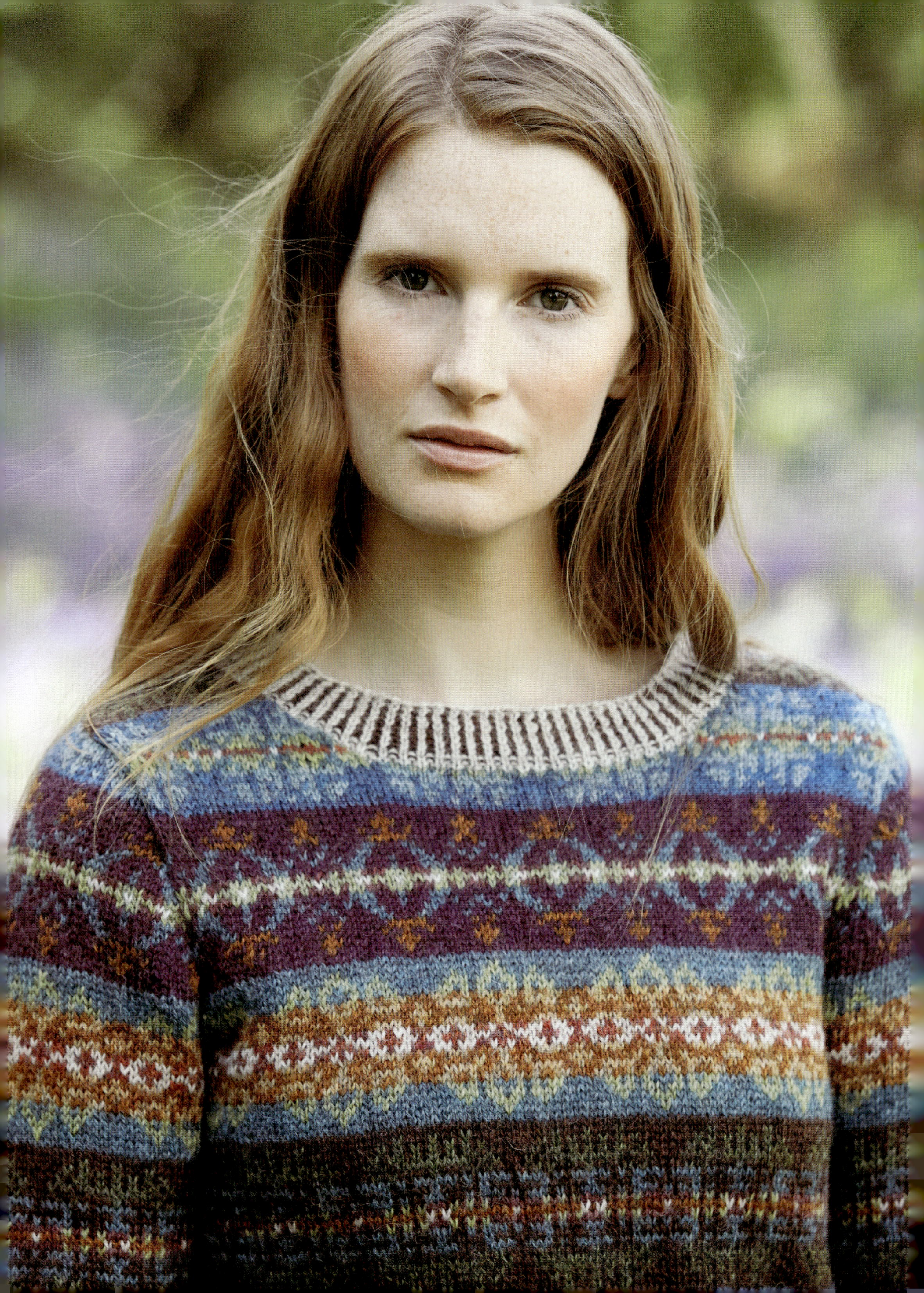

WILDWOOD

OAK

...is another Fair Isle design inspired by Eastern European folk art. OAK is a semi-fitted cardigan with extended shaped fronts that can be worn loose as styled or fastened with a beautiful pin.

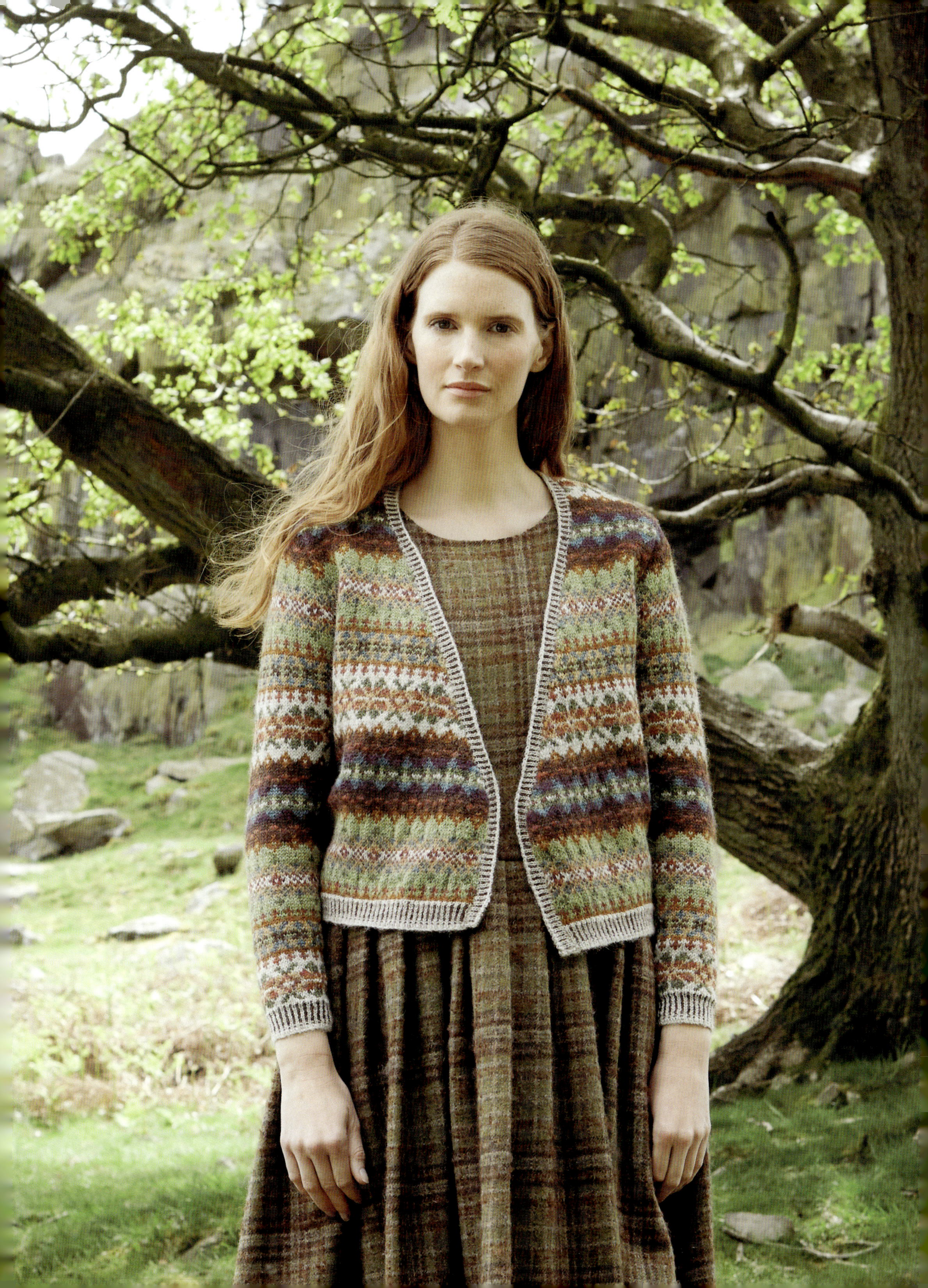

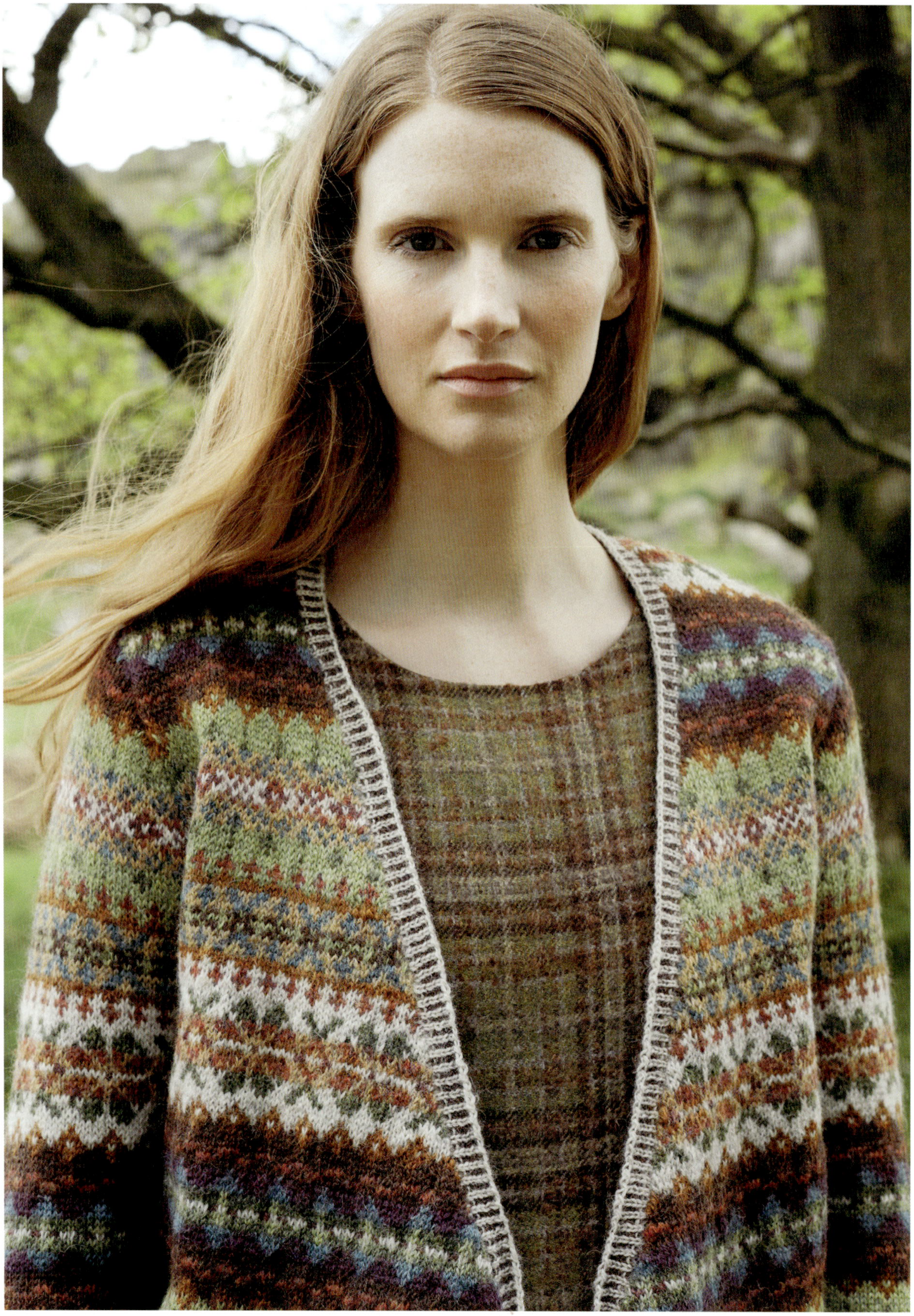

WILDWOOD

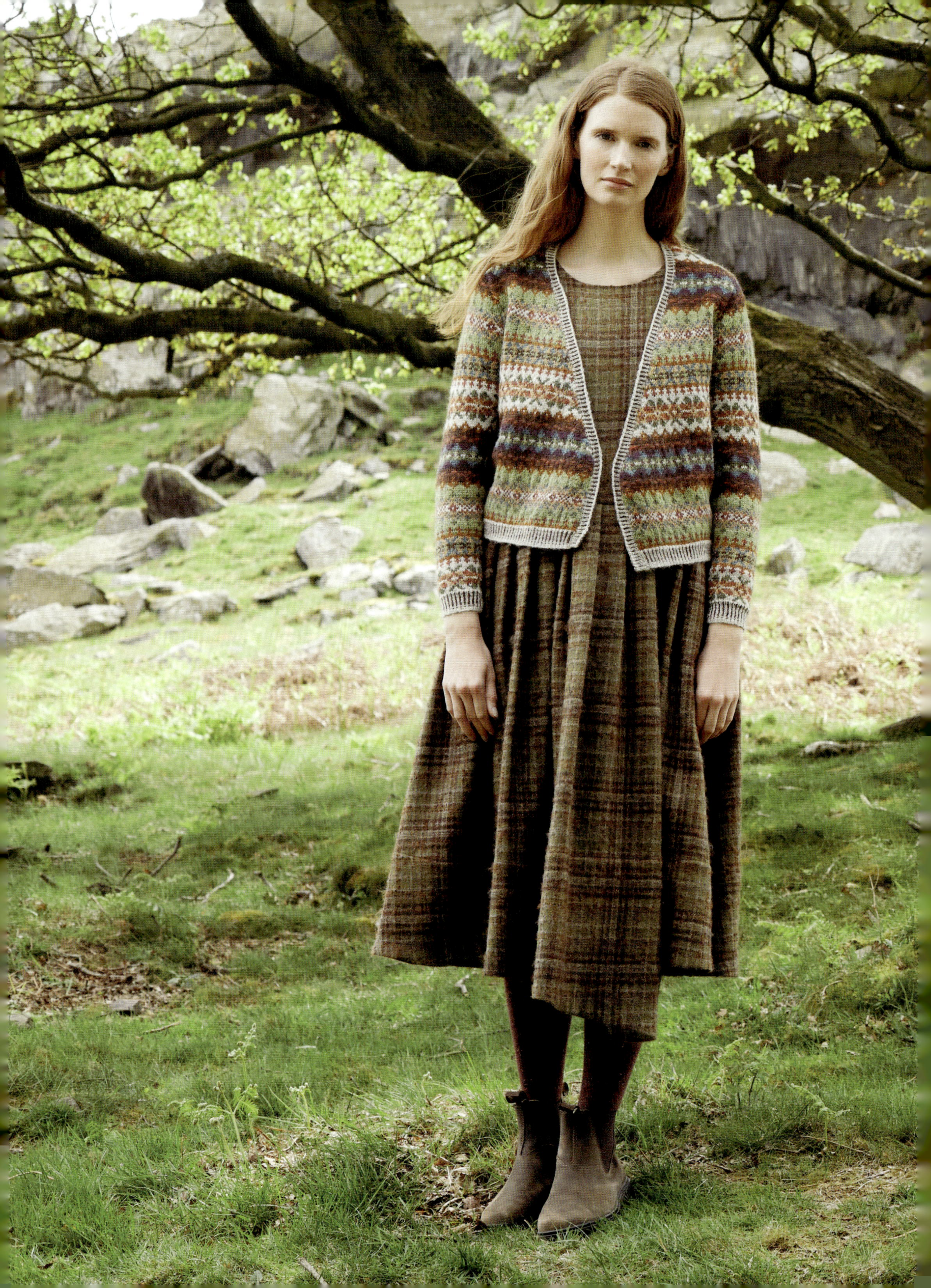

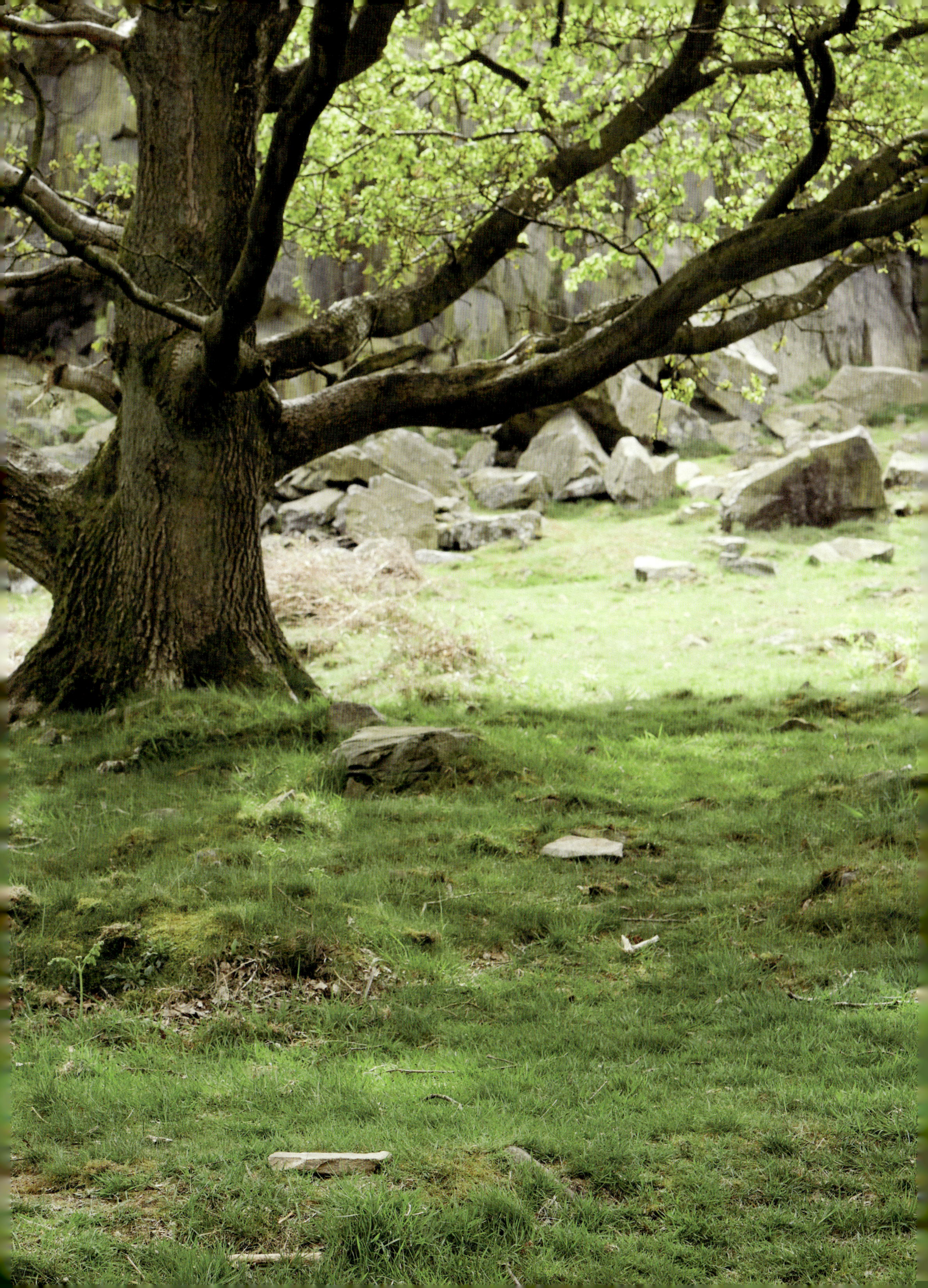

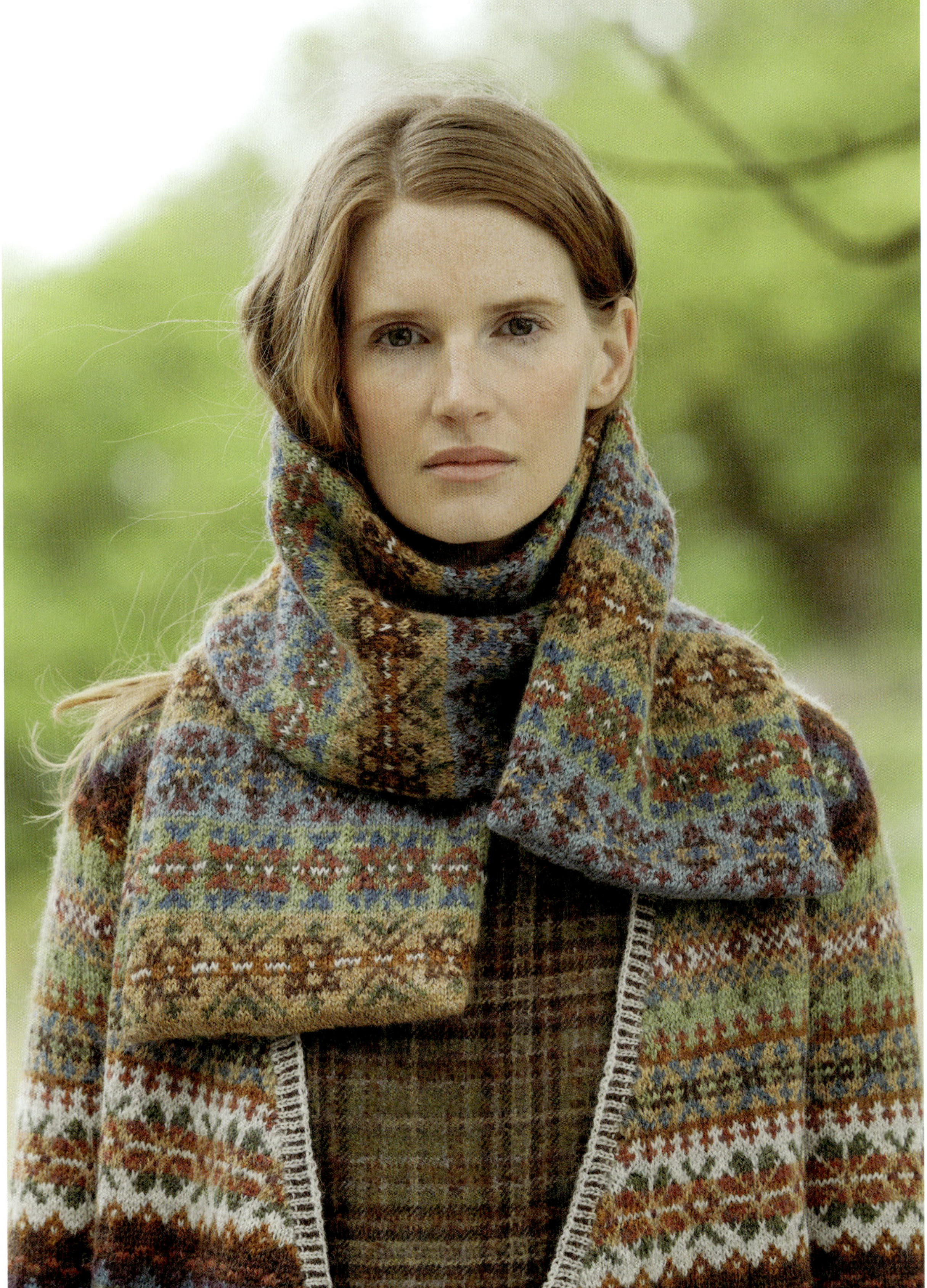

MAPLE SCARF

This pretty Fair Isle scarf inspired by ornamental design is entirely knitted in the round and will certainly keep you warm on the coldest of winter days. It can easily be shortened in length to create a beautiful cowl.

WILDWOOD

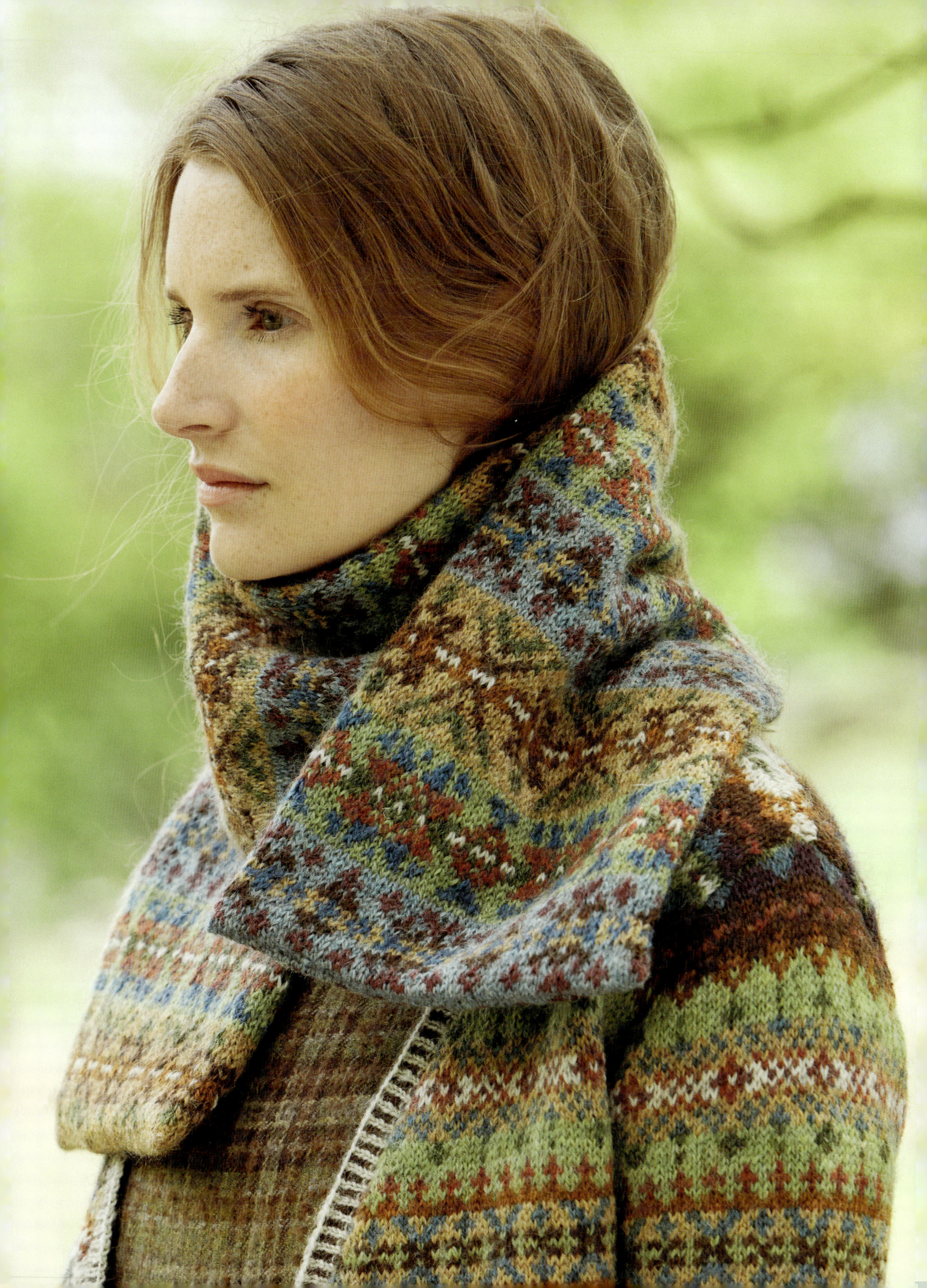

BIRCH

Knitted entirely in the round, this beautiful simple Fair Isle yoke design is a perfect project for knitters venturing into Fair Isle garment knitting for the first time.

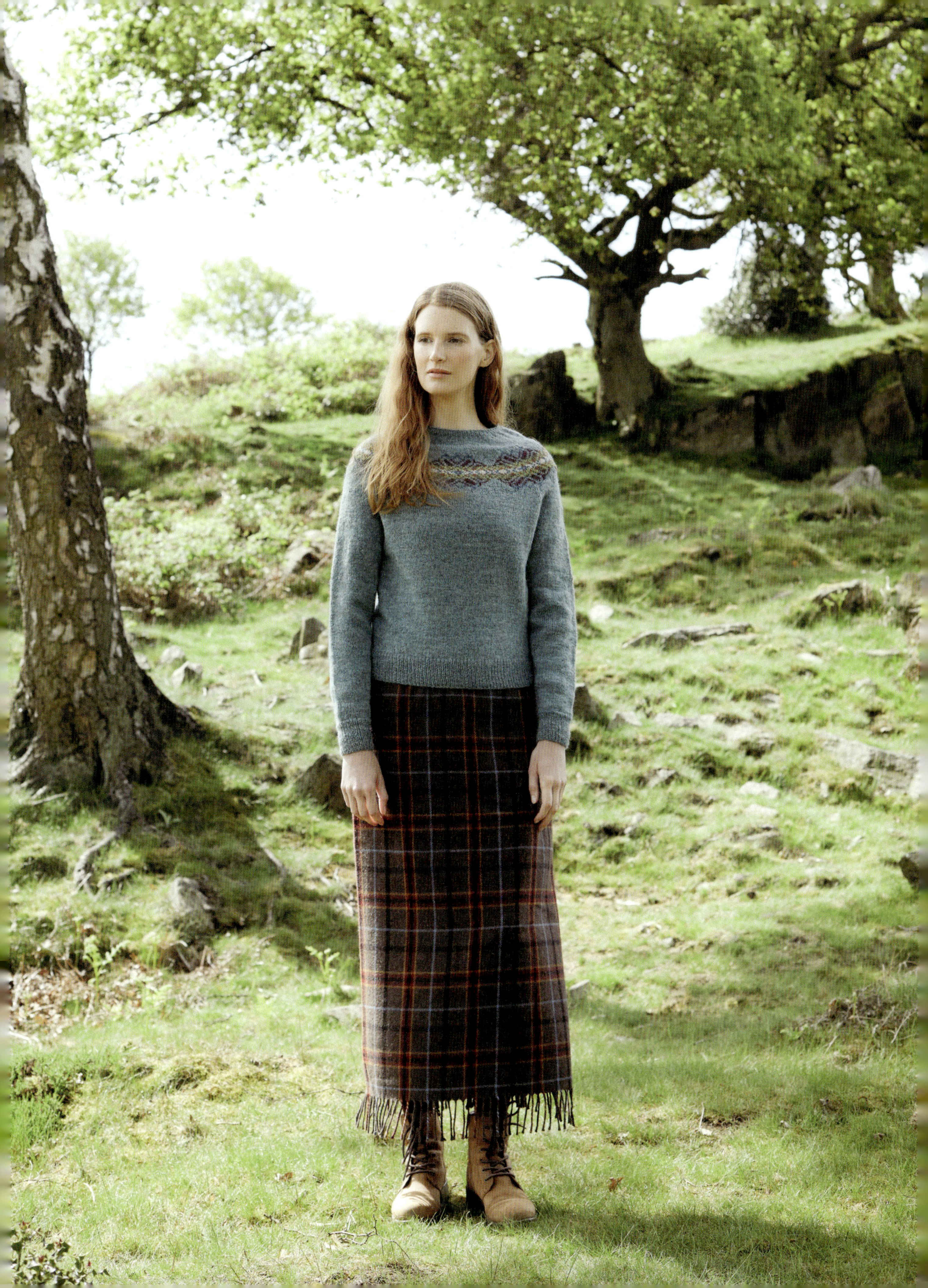

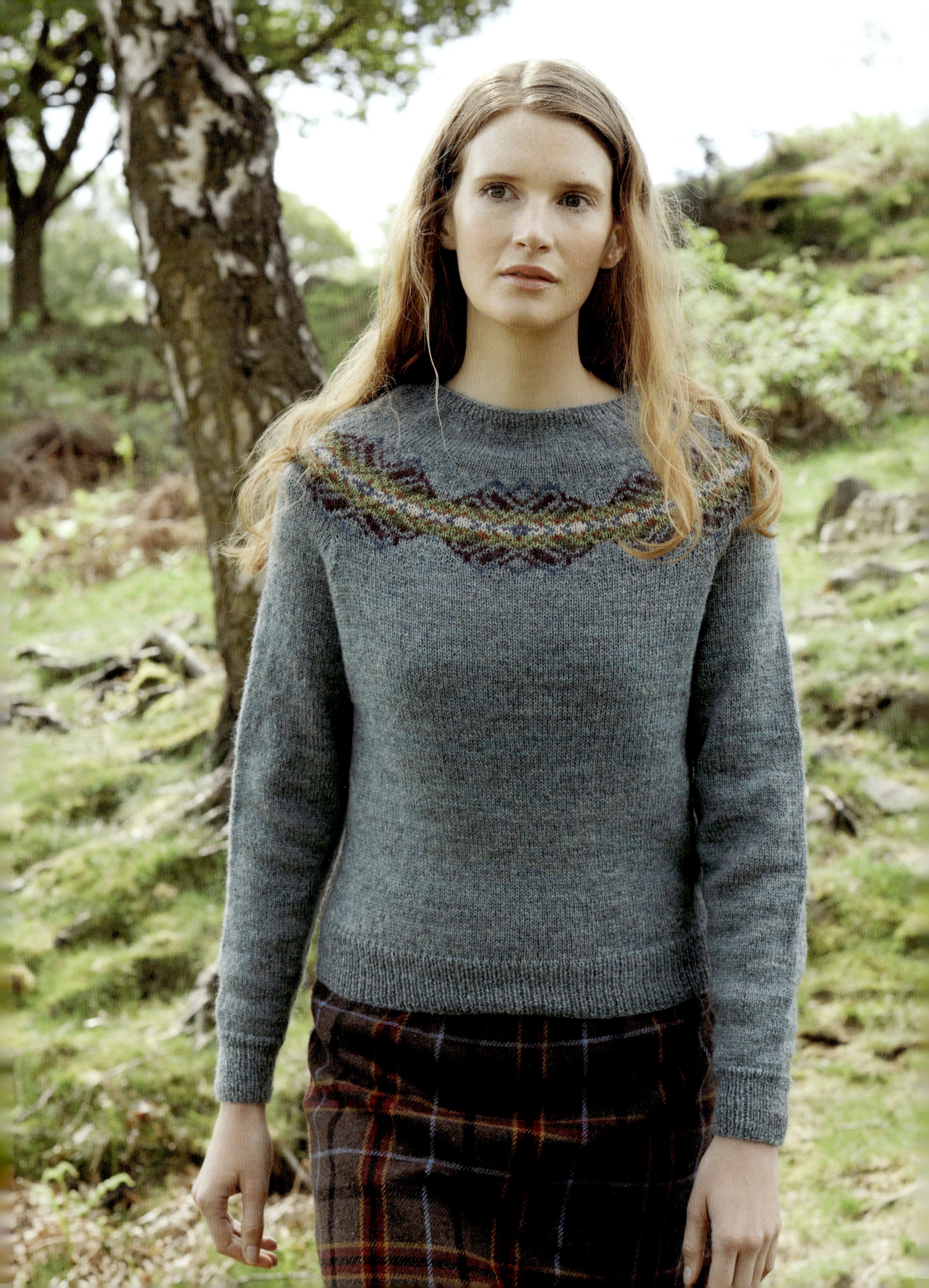

WILDWOOD

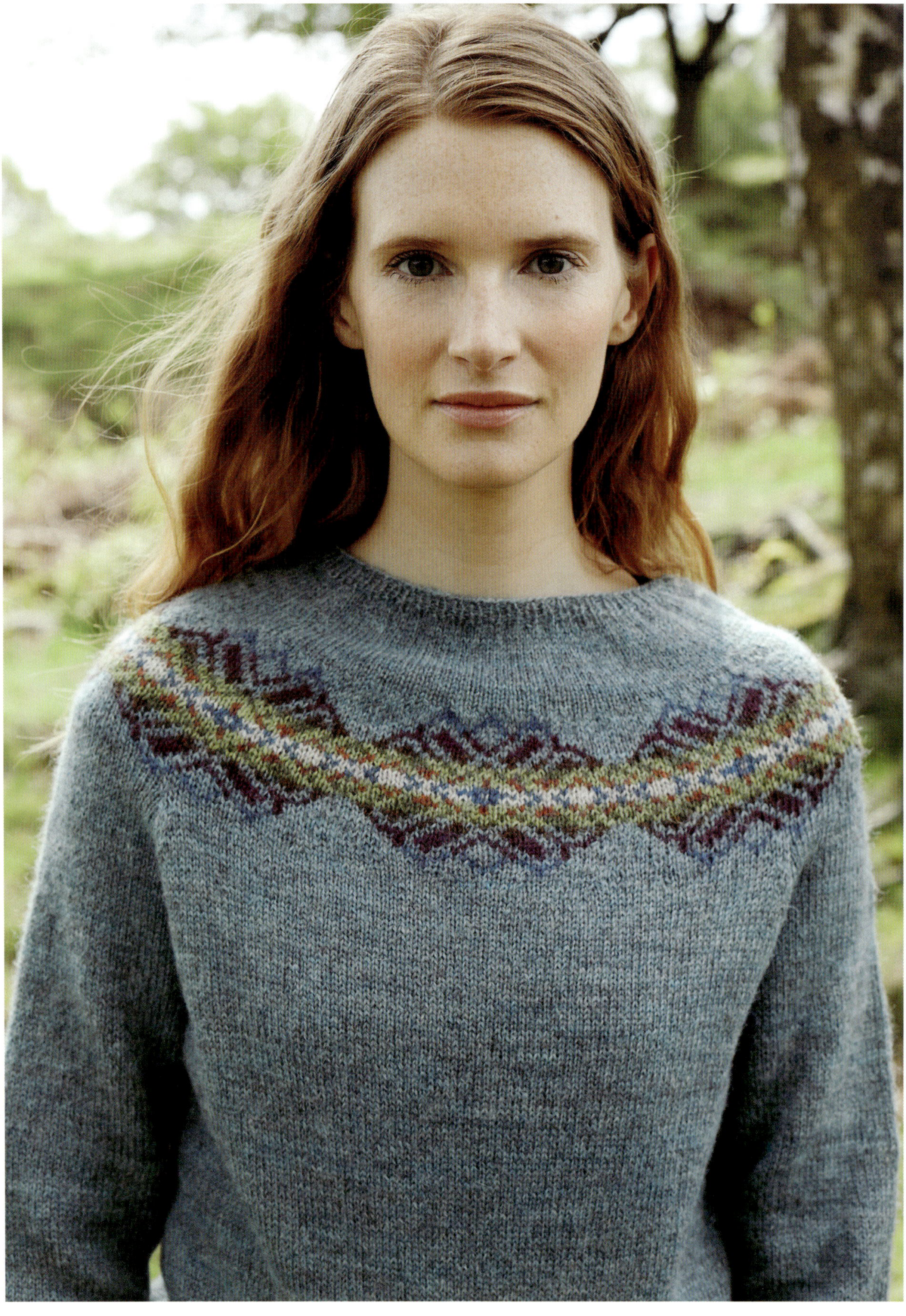

WILDWOOD

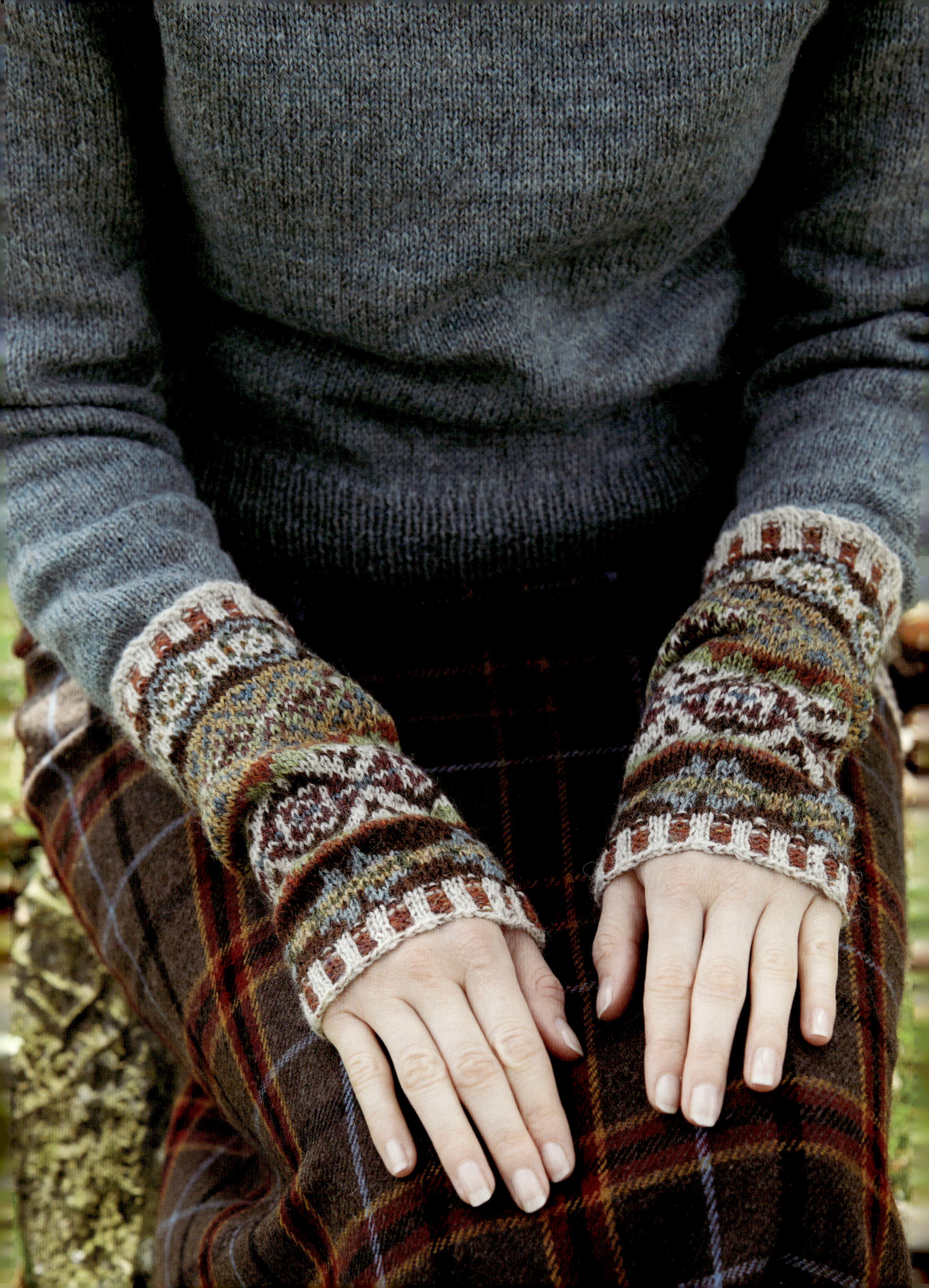

SYCAMORE ARMWARMERS

These pretty traditional Fair Isle armwarmers are fun and easy to knit. With instructions for both flat and knitting in the round, this design is easily achievable by the novice Fair Isle knitter.

WILDWOOD

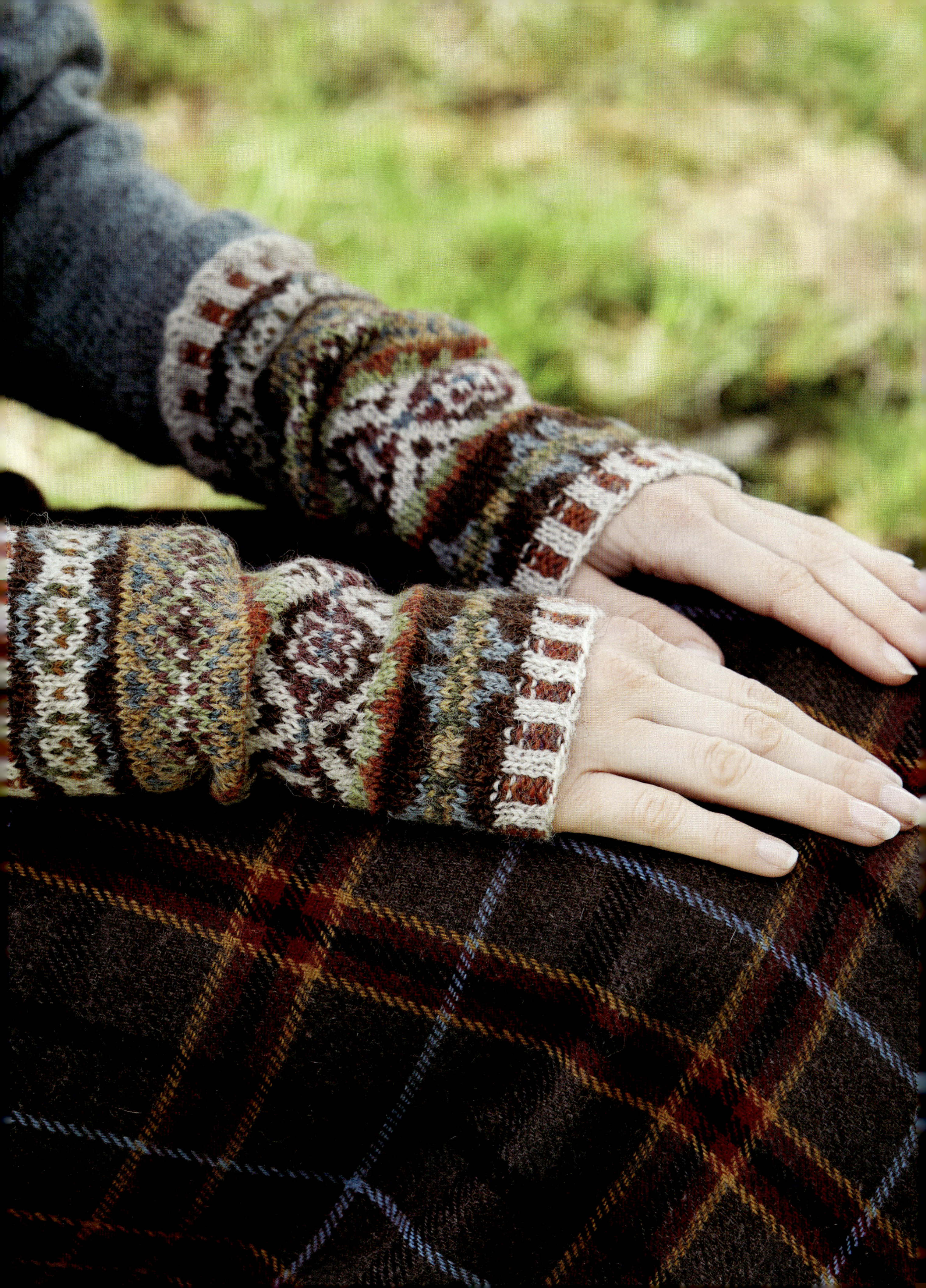

CHESTNUT

Using eight shades of BRITISH BREEDS, this beautiful traditional Fair Isle cardigan is knitted flat and will be perfect combined with your favourite tweed or tartan skirt.

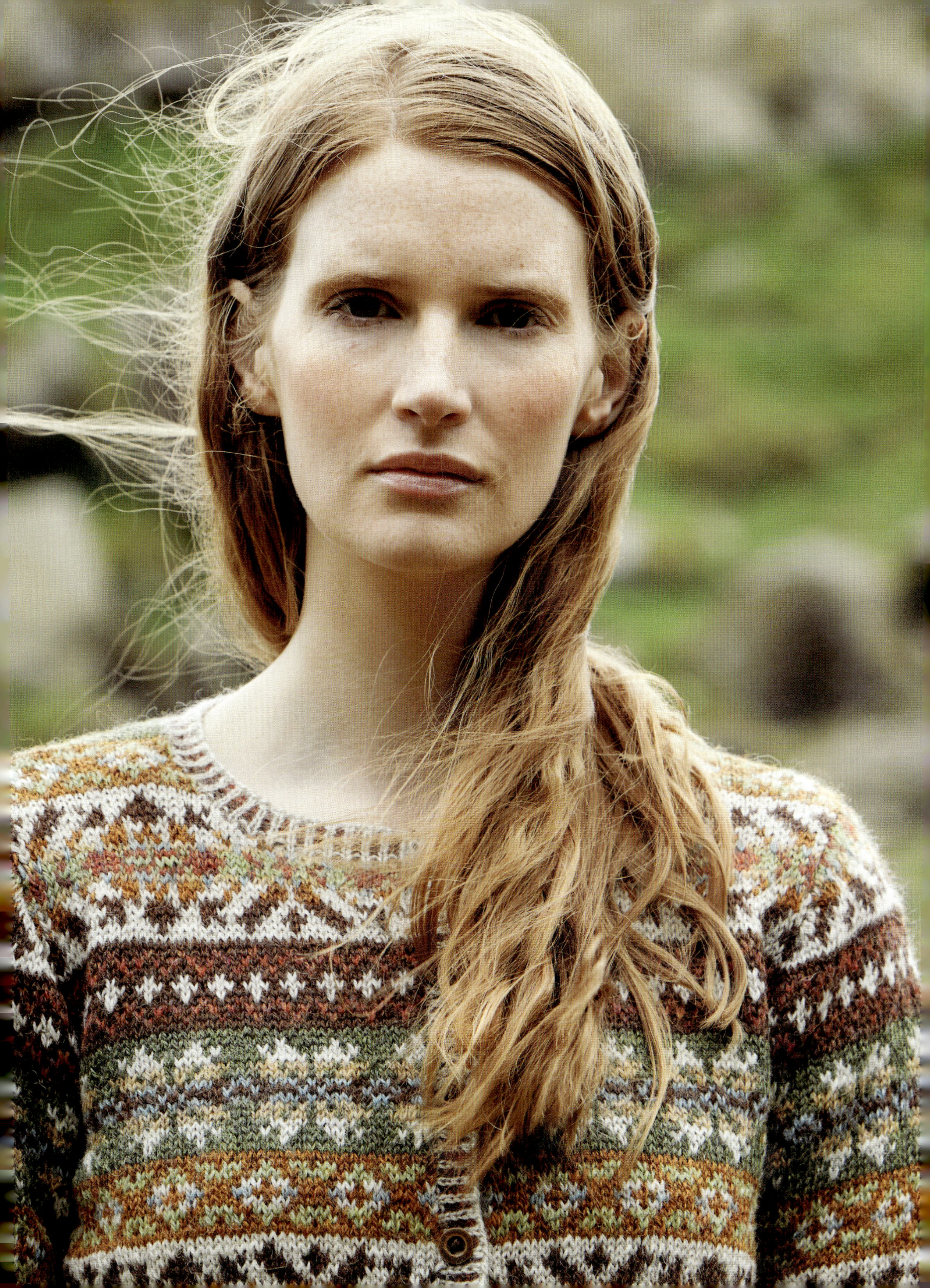

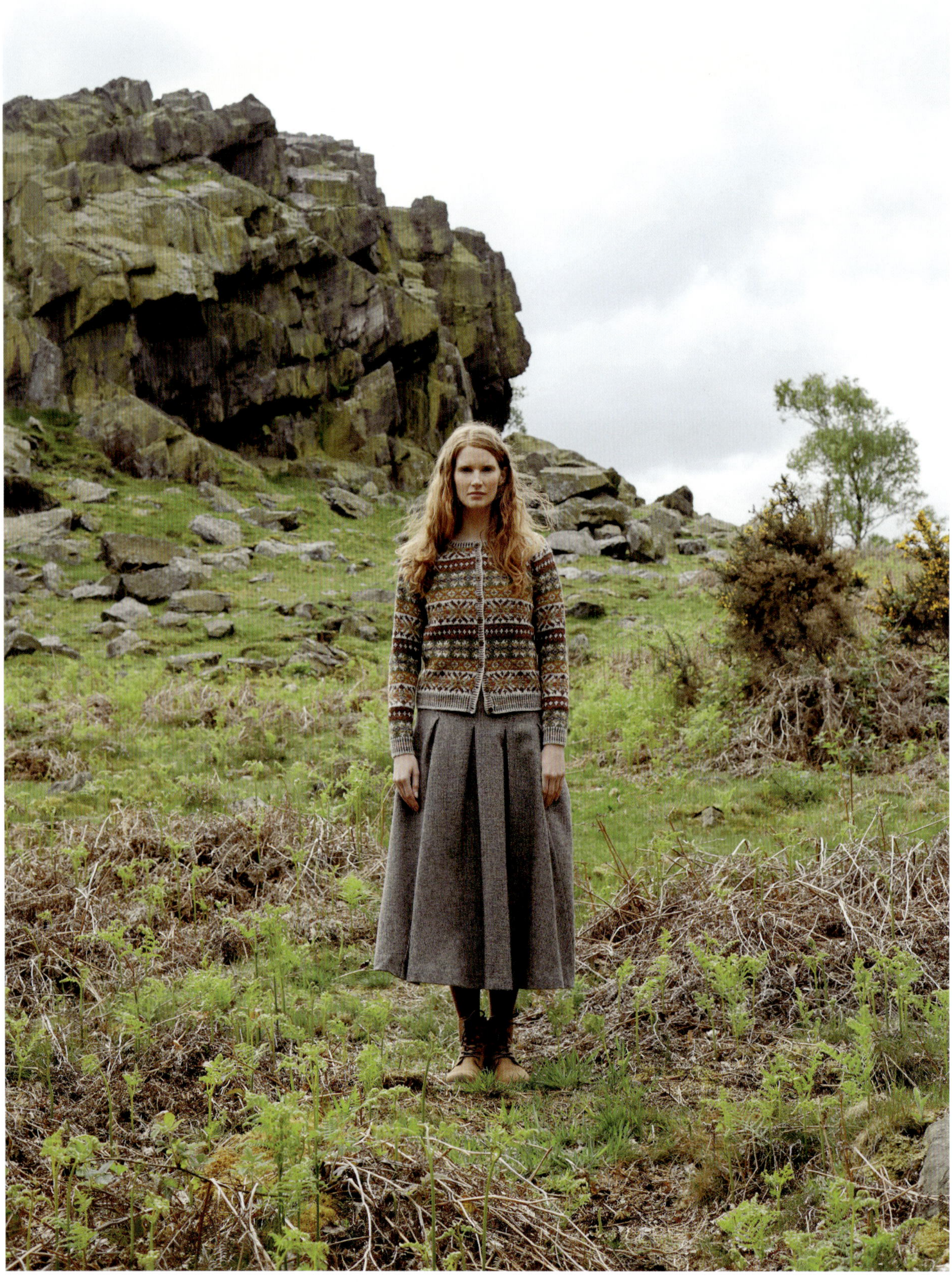

WILDWOOD

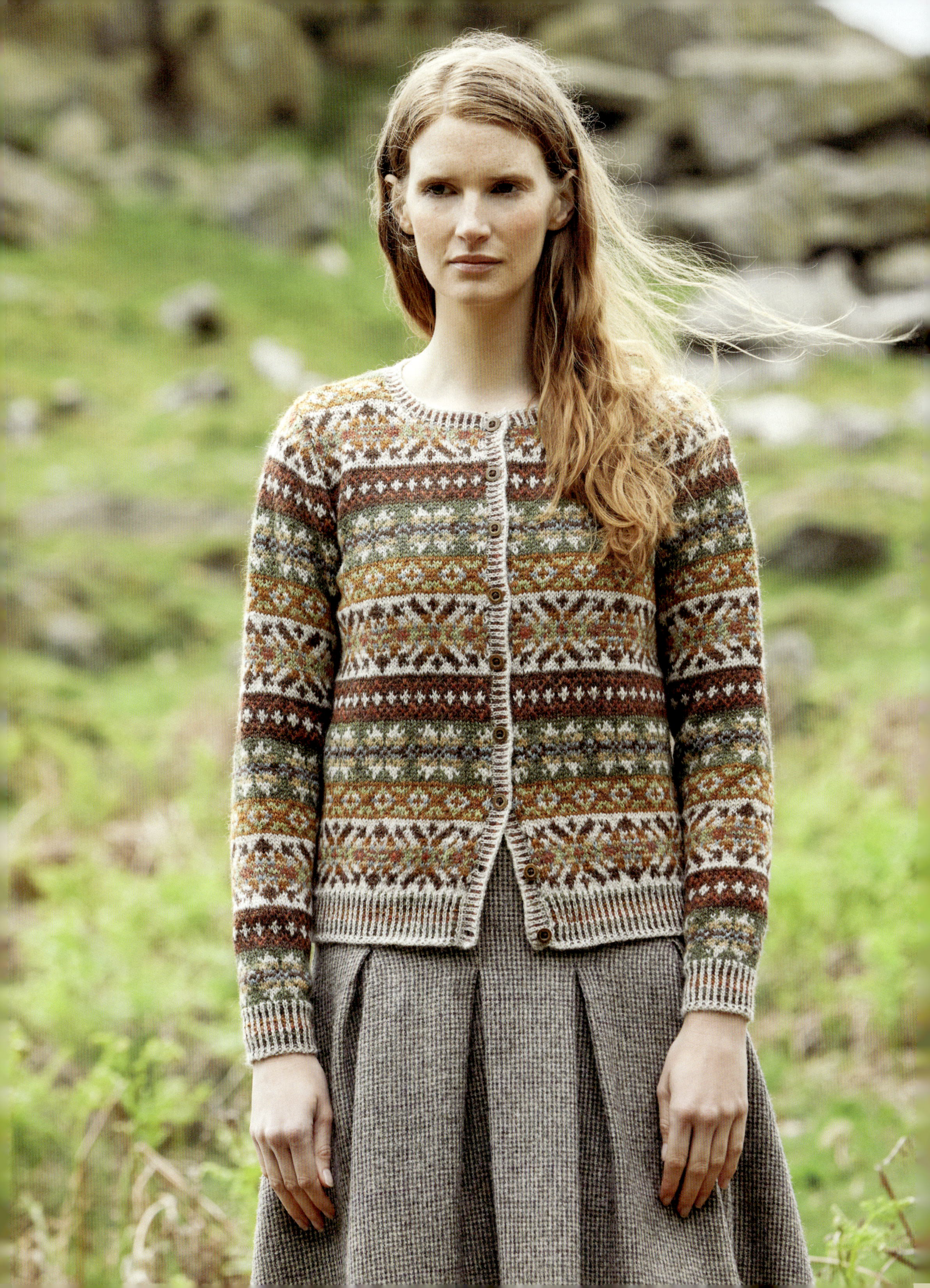

WILDWOOD

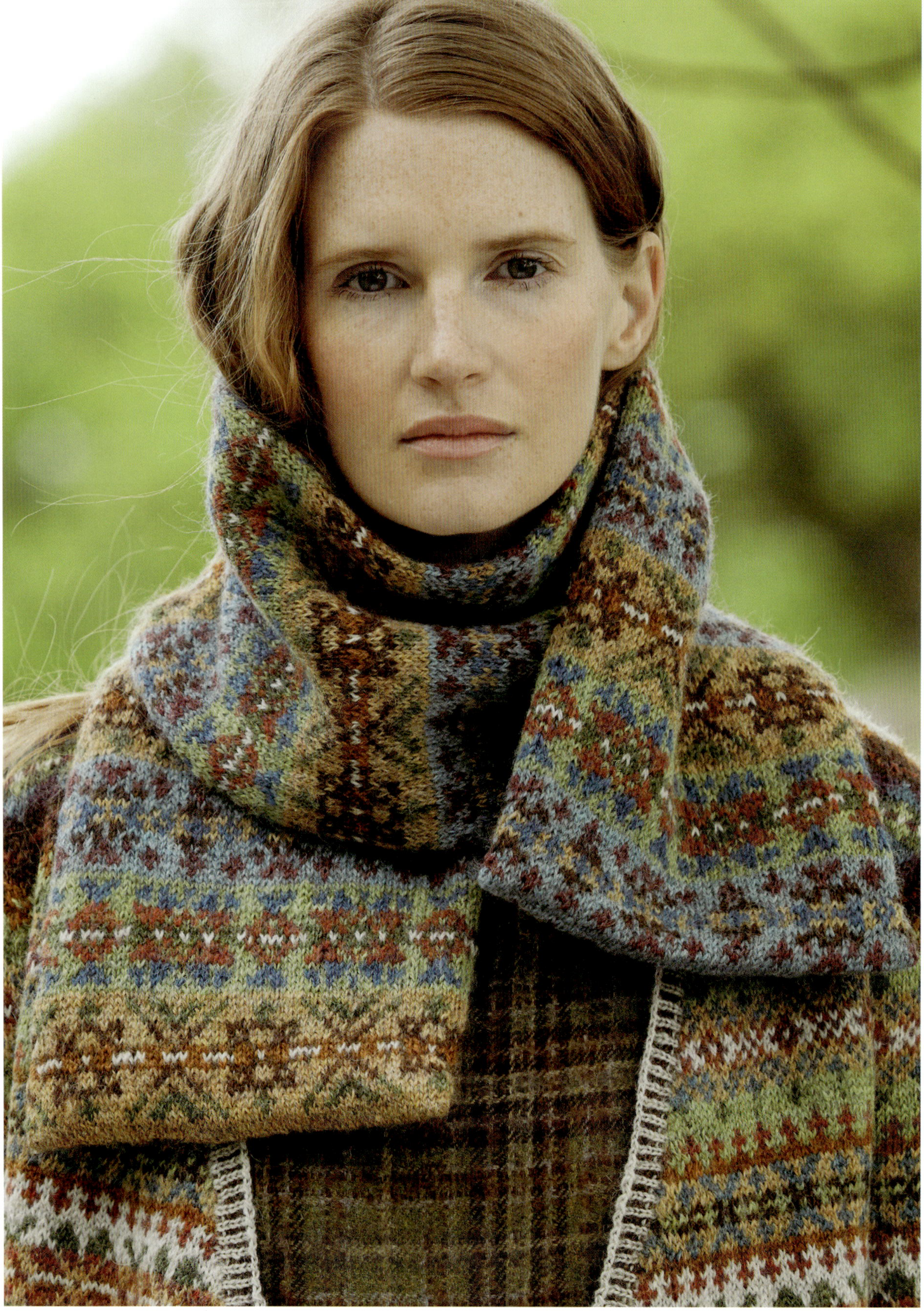

WILDWOOD

GALLERY

HAWTHORN
Main Image Pages 8, 9, 10, 11 & 110
Pattern Page 66

WALNUT TAM
Main Image Pages 12, 13, 14 & 15
Pattern Page 82

HOLLY
Main Image Pages 17, 18, 19 & 21
Pattern Page 69

YEW
Main Image Pages 6, 22, 24, 25, 26 & 27
Pattern Page 76

ROWAN COWL
Main Image Pages 29, 30 & 31
Pattern Page 80

WILD ROSE
Main Image Pages 5, 32, 33, 34, 35, 36 & 37
Pattern Page 94

OAK
Main Image Pages 39, 40, 42 & 43
Pattern Page 86

MAPLE SCARF
Main Image Pages 44, 47 & 64
Pattern Page 74

BIRCH
Main Image Pages 49, 50, 51 & 52
Pattern Page 72

SYCAMORE ARMWARMERS
Main Image Pages 54, 56 & 57
Pattern Page 84

CHESTNUT
Main Image Pages 58, 59, 60, 62 & 63
Pattern Page 90

65

HAWTHORN

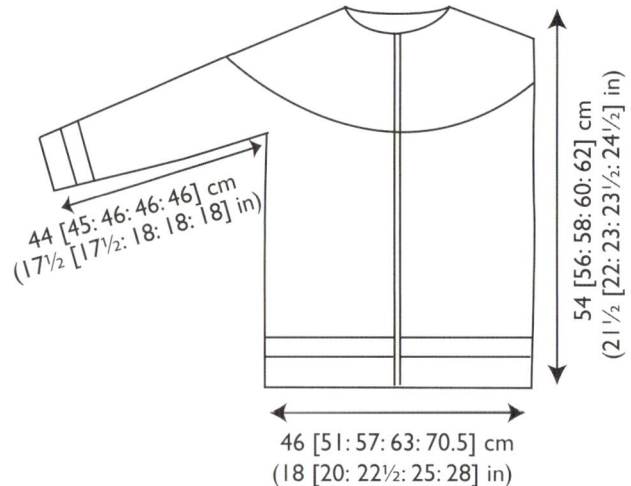

44 [45: 46: 46: 46] cm
(17½ [17½: 18: 18: 18] in)

54 [56: 58: 60: 62] cm
(21½ [22: 23: 23½: 24½] in)

46 [51: 57: 63: 70.5] cm
(18 [20: 22½: 25: 28] in)

	S	M	L	XL	XXL	
To fit bust	81-86	91-97	102-107	112-117	122-127	cm
	32-34	36-38	40-42	44-46	48-50	in

Marie Wallin British Breeds
A	Raw	11	13	14	15	17	x 25gm
B	Mulberry	1	1	1	1	1	x 25gm
C	Rose	1	1	1	1	1	x 25gm
D	Mallard	1	2	2	2	2	x 25gm
E	Lime Flower	1	1	1	2	2	x 25gm
F	Chestnut	1	1	1	1	1	x 25gm
G	Russet	1	1	1	1	1	x 25gm
H	Wood	1	1	1	1	1	x 25gm
I	Dark Apple	1	1	1	1	1	x 25gm
J	Quince	1	1	1	1	1	x 25gm

Needles
1 pair 2¼mm (no 13) (US 1) needles
2¼mm (no 13) (US 1) circular needle
2¾mm (no 12) (US 2) circular needle
3¼mm (no 10) (US 3) circular needle
Set of 4 double-pointed 2¼mm (no 13) (US 1) needles
Set of 4 double-pointed 2¾mm (no 12) (US 2) needles
Set of 4 double-pointed 3¼mm (no 10) (US 3) needles
2.50mm (no 12) (US B1/C2) crochet hook

Extras – Fine woven ribbon (to cover steek on inside)

Buttons – 8 x TGB2307 15mm from Textile Garden, see information page for contact details.

Tension
28 sts and 36 rounds to 10 cm measured over plain st st using 2¾mm (US 2) needles. 28 sts and 29 rounds to 10 cm measured over patterned st st using 3¼mm (US 3) needles.

Pattern note: Refer to steeking feature for how to cut the steeks.

BODY (knitted in one piece, with front opening edge steeked afterwards)
Using 2¼mm (US 1) circular needle and yarn A cast on 268 [296: 328: 364: 404] sts.
Taking care not to twist cast-on edge, work in rounds as folls:
Round 1 (RS): K5, *K1, P1, rep from * to last 5 sts, K5.
Place marker on first st of round just knitted to denote beg and end of rounds – this marker "sits" at centre front and will be the steeked st later. The centre front 9 sts (the marked steeking st and 4 sts each side of this st) will be used for the steek – place 2 further markers, one on each side of these 9 sts.
Last round forms rib.
Work in rib for a further 18 rounds.
Change to 2¾mm (US 2) circular needle.
Work in st st (K every round) for 3 rounds.
Next round: K22 [74: 27: 30: 101], M1, (K45 [149: 55: 61: 203], M1) 5 [1: 5: 5: 1] times, K21 [73: 26: 29: 100]. 274 [298: 334: 370: 406] sts.
Change to 3¼mm (US 3) circular needle.
Beg and ending rounds as indicated, joining in and breaking off

YOKE CHART

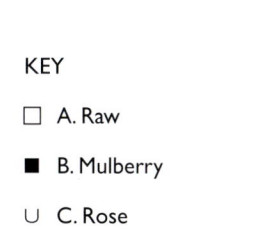

12 st pattern rep

KEY

- ☐ A. Raw
- ■ B. Mulberry
- ∪ C. Rose
- ● D. Mallard
- ○ E. Lime Flower
- ▲ F. Chestnut
- · G. Russet
- ◢ H. Wood
- × I. Dark Apple
- | J. Quince

BODY CHART

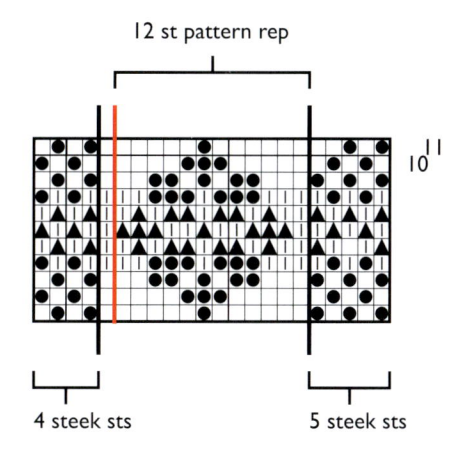

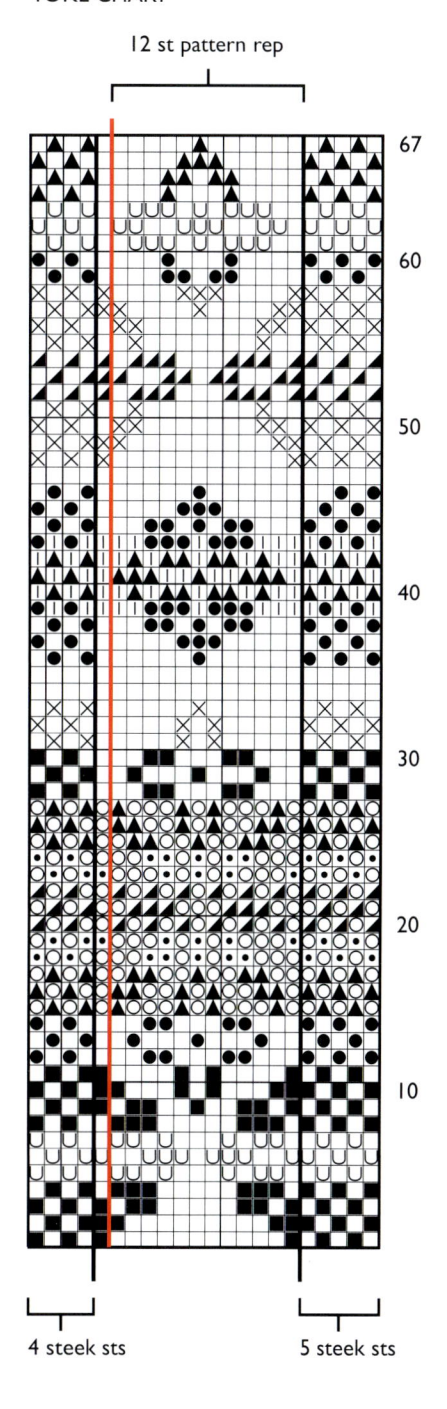

12 st pattern rep

4 steek sts | 5 steek sts

4 steek sts | 5 steek sts

SLEEVE CHART

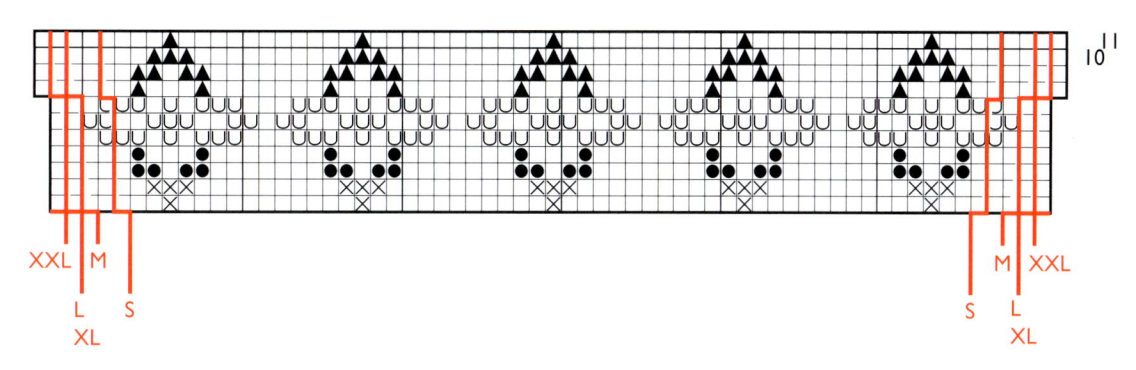

XXL M
L   S
XL

M XXL
S L
   XL

67

colours as required, using the **fairisle** technique as described on the information page and repeating the 12 st patt repeat 22 [24: 27: 30: 33] times around each round, cont in patt from chart for body, which is worked entirely in st st (K every round), as folls:
Work rounds 1 to 11.
Change to 2¾mm (US 2) circular needle.
Break off contrasts and cont using yarn A only.
Next round: K21 [73: 26: 29: 100], K2tog, (K44 [148: 54: 60: 202], K2tog) 5 [1: 5: 5: 1] times, K21 [73: 26: 29: 100].
268 [296: 328: 364: 404] sts.
Now work in st st throughout as folls:
Cont straight until body meas 28 [29: 30: 31: 32] cm.
Next round: K marked centre front st and next 64 [71: 79: 88: 98] sts and slip these 65 [72: 80: 89: 99] sts onto a holder for right front, K10 and slip these 10 sts onto another holder for right underarm, K119 [133: 149: 167: 187] and slip these sts onto another holder for back, K10 and slip these 10 sts onto another holder for left underarm, K rem 64 [71: 79: 88: 98] sts and slip these sts onto another holder for left front.
Break yarn.

SLEEVES
Using set of 4 double-pointed 2¼mm (US 1) needles and yarn A cast on 53 [57: 59: 59: 61] sts.
Taking care not to twist cast-on edge, work in rounds as folls:
Round 1 (RS): P1, *K1, P1, rep from * to end.
This round forms rib.
Place marker on first st of round just knitted to denote beg and end of rounds – this marker "sits" along sleeve "seam".
Work in rib for a further 18 rounds.
Change to double-pointed 2¾mm (US 2) needles.
Now working in st st (K every round), cont as folls:
Work 4 rounds.
Change to 3¼mm (US 3) double pointed needles. Beg and ending rounds as indicated, joining in and breaking off colours as required, and using the **fairisle** technique as described on the information page, cont in patt from chart for sleeve, which is worked entirely in st st (K every round), as folls:
Work rounds 1 to 11, inc 1 st at each end of first and foll 6th round, taking inc sts into patt. 57 [61: 63: 63: 65] sts.
Change to 2¾mm (US 2) double pointed needles. Break off contrasts and cont using yarn A only.
Work 1 round.
Next round (RS): K2, M1, K to last st, M1, K1. 59 [63: 65: 65: 67] sts.
Working all sleeve increases as set by last round, cont as folls:
Inc 1 st at each end of 6th and every foll 6th round to 75 [75: 73: 89: 99] sts, then on every foll 8th round until there are 89 [93: 95: 99: 103] sts.
Cont straight until sleeve meas 44 [45: 46: 46: 46] cm.
Next round: K5 and slip these sts onto a holder (for underarm), K to last 5 sts, K rem 5 sts and slip these 5 sts onto same holder as first 5 sts (so there are 10 sts on underarm holder).
Break yarn and leave rem 79 [83: 85: 89: 93] sts on another holder.

YOKE
Pattern note: when working the part of the fairisle band that sits over the shoulders, strand a little more loosely than normal so as not to restrict the band when being worn.

With RS facing, using 2¾mm (US 2) circular needle and yarn A, work across all sts from holders as folls: K across 65 [72: 80: 89: 99] sts on right front holder, place marker on needle, K 79 [83: 85: 89: 93] sts on right sleeve holder, place 2nd marker on needle, K 119 [133: 149: 167: 187] sts on back holder, place 3rd marker on needle, K 79 [83: 85: 89: 93] sts on left sleeve holder, place 4th marker on needle, then K 64 [71: 79: 88: 98] sts on left front holder. 406 [442: 478: 522: 570] sts.
Place marker on first st of round just knitted to denote beg and end of rounds – this marker "sits" at centre front and will be the steeked st later.
There are now 5 markers – one at centre front and 4 more denoting raglan "seam" positions.
Working in st st throughout, cont as folls:
Work 1 round.
Next round: K to within 2 sts of right front raglan "seam" marker, K2tog (for right front raglan armhole dec), slip marker onto right needle, sl 1, K1, psso (for first raglan dec of right sleeve), K to within 2 sts of right back raglan "seam" marker, K2tog (for second raglan dec of right sleeve), slip marker onto right needle, sl 1, K1, psso (for right back raglan armhole dec), K to within 2 sts of left back raglan "seam" marker, K2tog (for left back raglan armhole dec), slip marker onto right needle, sl 1, K1, psso (for first raglan dec of left sleeve), K to within 2 sts of left front raglan "seam" marker, K2tog (for second raglan dec of left sleeve), slip marker onto right needle, sl 1, K1, psso (for left front raglan armhole dec), K to end. 398 [434: 470: 514: 562] sts.
Rep last 2 rounds 3 [5: 6: 8: 10] times more.
374 [394: 422: 450: 482] sts.
(Note: As number of sts decreases, change from circular needle to set of 4 double-pointed needles).
Remove all raglan "seam" markers but leave marker on centre front st.
Next round: K45 [394: 51: 28: 60], (K2tog) 1 [0: 1: 1: 1] times, (K92 [0: 104: 54: 118], K2tog) 3 [0: 3: 7: 3] times, K45 [0: 51: 28: 60]. 370 [394: 418: 442: 478] sts.
Change to 3¼mm (US 3) circular needle.
Beg and ending rounds as indicated and repeating the 12 st patt repeat 30 [32: 34: 36: 39] times around each round, cont in patt from chart for yoke as folls:
Work rounds 1 to 34.
Round 35: Using yarn A, K17 [5: 20: 5: 29], (K1, K2tog, K1 [2: 1: 2: 1], sl 1, K1, psso, K1) 48 [48: 54: 54: 60] times, K17 [5: 20: 5: 29]. 274 [298: 310: 334: 358] sts.
Work rounds 36 to 46, repeating the 12 st patt repeat 22 [24: 25: 27: 29] times around each round.
Round 47: Using yarn A, K12 [6: 12: 6: 18], sl 1, K1, psso, (K1, sl 1, K1, psso) 83 [95: 95: 107: 107] times, K11 [5: 11: 5: 17]. 190 [202: 214: 226: 250] sts.
Work rounds 48 to 67, repeating the 12 st patt repeat 15 [16: 17: 18: 20] times around each round.
All 67 rounds of chart are now completed. Break off contrasts and cont using yarn A only as folls:
Next round: K8 [6: 7: 6: 8], (K2tog, K1, sl 1, K1, psso) 35 [38: 40: 43: 47] times, K7 [6: 7: 5: 7]. 120 [126: 134: 140: 156] sts.
Work neckband
Change to 4 double-pointed 2¼mm (US 1) needles.
Work in rib as given for body for 5 rounds.
Cast off in rib.

MAKING UP
Press as described on the information page.
Following instructions on information page, cut centre front steek.
Button band
With RS facing, using 2¼mm (US 1) needles and yarn A, pick up and knit 167 [173: 179: 185: 191] sts evenly down left front opening edge, from top of neckband to cast-on edge.
Row 1 (WS): K1, *P1, K1, rep from * to end.

Row 2: K2, *P1, K1, rep from * to last st, K1.
These 2 rows form rib with first and last st of every row worked as a K st.
Keeping sts correct, cont as folls:
Cast off 36 sts at beg of next row. 131 [137: 143: 149: 155] sts.
Work in rib for a further 2 rows, ending with RS facing for next row.
Cast off in rib.

Buttonhole band
With RS facing, using 2¼mm (US 1) needles and yarn A, pick up and knit 167 [173: 179: 185: 191] sts evenly up right front opening edge, from cast-on edge to top of neckband.

Beg with row 1, work in rib as given for button band as folls:
Work 1 row, ending with RS facing for next row.
Row 2 (RS): Cast off first 36 sts, rib until there are 6 [5: 5: 4: 4] sts on right needle after cast-off, *yrn, work 2 tog (to make a buttonhole), rib 15 [16: 17: 18: 19], rep from * 6 times more, yrn, work 2 tog (to make 8th buttonhole), rib 4 [4: 3: 3: 2].
Work in rib for a further 3 rows, ending with RS facing for next row.
Cast off in rib.
Join underarm seams by grafting together sets of 10 sts on underarm holders. Sew on buttons.
See information page for finishing instructions.

HOLLY ● ● ●

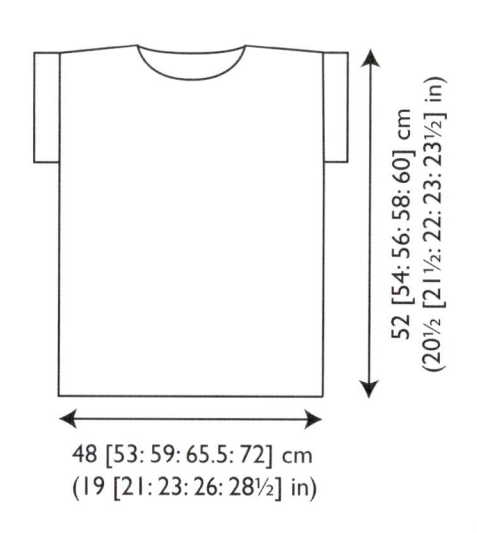

48 [53: 59: 65.5: 72] cm
(19 [21: 23: 26: 28½] in)

52 [54: 56: 58: 60] cm
(20½ [21½: 22: 23: 23½] in)

	S	M	L	XL	XXL	
To fit bust	81-86	91-97	102-107	112-117	122-127	cm
	32-34	36-38	40-42	44-46	48-50	in

Marie Wallin British Breeds

A	Raw	7	8	9	10	11	x 25gm
B	Chestnut	1	1	1	1	1	x 25gm
C	Eau de Nil	1	1	1	1	2	x 25gm
D	Wood	1	1	1	1	1	x 25gm
E	Mallard	1	1	2	2	2	x 25gm
F	Quince	1	1	1	1	2	x 25gm
G	Dark Apple	1	1	1	1	1	x 25gm
H	Mulberry	1	1	1	1	2	x 25gm
I	Lime Flower	1	1	1	1	1	x 25gm
J	Russet	1	1	1	1	1	x 25gm
K	Rose	1	1	1	1	1	x 25gm

Needles
1 pair 2¾mm (no 12) (US 2) needles
1 pair 3¼mm (no 10) (US 3) needles

Tension
28 sts and 29 rows to 10 cm measured over patterned st st using 3¼mm (US 3) needles.

BACK
Using 2¾mm (US 2) needles and yarn A cast on
135 [149: 165: 183: 201] sts.
Row 1 (RS): K1, *P1, K1, rep from * to end.
Row 2: P1, *K1, P1, rep from * to end.
These 2 rows form rib.
Cont in rib until work meas 7 cm, ending with RS facing for next row.
Change to 3¼mm (US 3) needles.
Beg and ending rows as indicated, using the **fairisle** technique as described on the information page and repeating the 74 row patt repeat throughout, cont in patt from chart, which is worked entirely in st st beg with a K row, as folls:
Work 2 rows, ending with RS facing for next row.
Inc 1 st at each end of next and 11 [10: 9: 10: 12] foll 4th rows, then on foll 8 [11: 15: 14: 12] alt rows, taking inc sts into patt. 175 [193: 215: 233: 251] sts.
Work 1 row, ending with RS facing for next row.
Place markers at both ends of last row (to denote base of armhole openings).
Cont straight until work meas 17 [18: 19: 20: 21] cm **from markers**, ending with RS facing for next row.
Shape shoulders
Keeping patt correct, cast off 5 [6: 7: 8: 9] sts at beg of next 2 [4: 4: 6: 10] rows, then 6 [7: 8: 9: 10] sts at beg of foll 10 [8: 8: 6: 2] rows. 105 [113: 123: 131: 141] sts.
Shape back neck
Next row (RS): Cast off 6 [7: 8: 9: 10] sts, patt until there are 22 [25: 28: 31: 34] sts on right needle and turn, leaving rem sts on a holder.
Work each side of neck separately.
Dec 1 st at neck edge of next 4 rows **and at same time** cast off 6 [7: 8: 9: 10] sts at beg of 2nd and foll alt row.
Work 1 row.
Cast off rem 6 [7: 8: 9: 10] sts.
With RS facing, slip centre 49 [49: 51: 51: 53] sts onto a holder (for neckband), rejoin yarns and patt to end.
Complete to match first side, reversing shapings.

FRONT
Work as given for back to beg of shoulder shaping, ending with RS facing for next row.
Sizes S, M, L and XL only
Shape shoulders
Keeping patt correct, cast off 5 [6: 7: 8: -] sts at beg of next 2 [4: 2: 2: -] rows, then 6 [0: 0: 0: -] sts at beg of foll 2 [0: 0: 0: -]

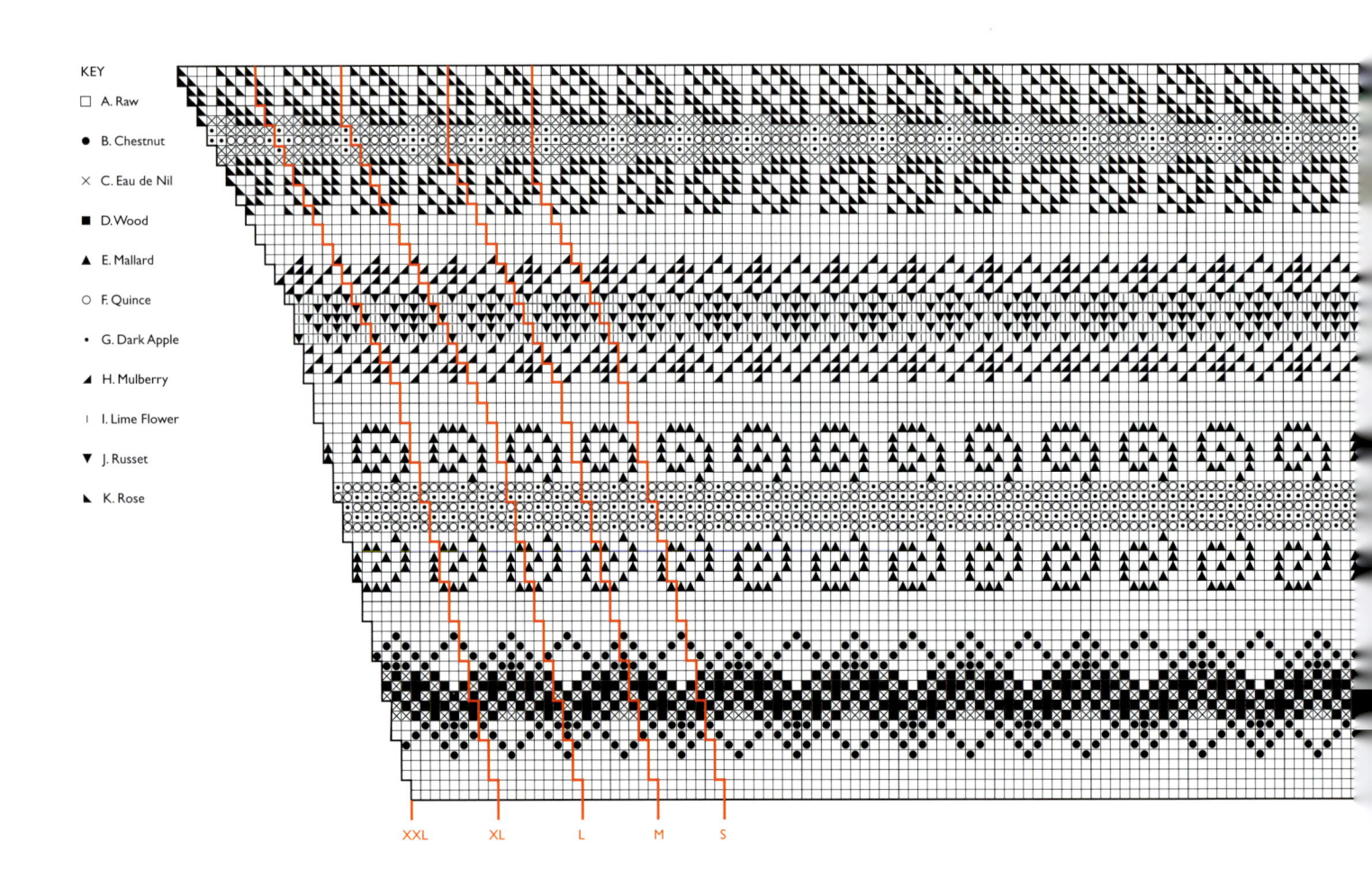

KEY
□ A. Raw
● B. Chestnut
× C. Eau de Nil
■ D. Wood
▲ E. Mallard
○ F. Quince
· G. Dark Apple
▲ H. Mulberry
| I. Lime Flower
▼ J. Russet
◣ K. Rose

rows. 153 [169: 201: 217: -] sts.
Shape front neck
Next row (RS): Cast off 6 [7: 7: 8: -] sts, patt until there are 50 [57: 73: 80: -] sts on right needle and turn, leaving rem sts on a holder.
Size XXL only
Shape shoulders and front neck
Next row (RS): Cast off 9 sts, patt until there are 96 sts on right needle and turn, leaving rem sts on a holder.
All sizes
Work each side of neck separately.
Keeping patt correct, cast off 6 [7: 8: 8: 9] sts at beg of 2nd and foll 5 [5: 6: 0: 3] alt rows, then - [-: -: 9: 10] sts at beg of foll - [-: -: 6: 4] alt rows **and at same time** dec 1 st at neck edge of next 6 rows, then on foll 2 [2: 3: 3: 4] alt rows.
Work 1 row.
Cast off rem 6 [7: 8: 9: 10] sts.
With RS facing, slip centre 41 sts onto a holder (for neckband), rejoin yarns and patt to end.
Complete to match first side, reversing shapings.

MAKING UP
Press as described on the information page.
Join right shoulder seam using back stitch, or mattress stitch if preferred.
Neckband
With RS facing, using 2¾mm (US 2) needles and yarn A, pick up and knit 15 [15: 17: 17: 19] sts down left side of front neck, K across 41 sts on front holder, pick up and knit 15 [15: 17: 17: 19] sts up right side of front neck, and 5 sts down right side of back neck, K across 49 [49: 51: 51: 53] sts on back holder inc 1 st at centre, then pick up and knit 5 sts up left side of back neck.
131 [131: 137: 137: 143] sts.
Beg with row 2, work in rib as given for back for 5 rows, ending with RS facing for next row.
Cast off in rib.
Join left shoulder and neckband seam.
Cuff borders (both alike)
With RS facing, using 2¾mm (US 2) needles and yarn A, pick up and knit 95 [101: 107: 113: 117] sts evenly along straight row-end edge of armhole opening between markers.
Beg with row 2, work in rib as given for back for 4 cm, ending with RS facing for next row.
Cast off in rib.
Join side and cuff border seams.
See information page for finishing instructions.

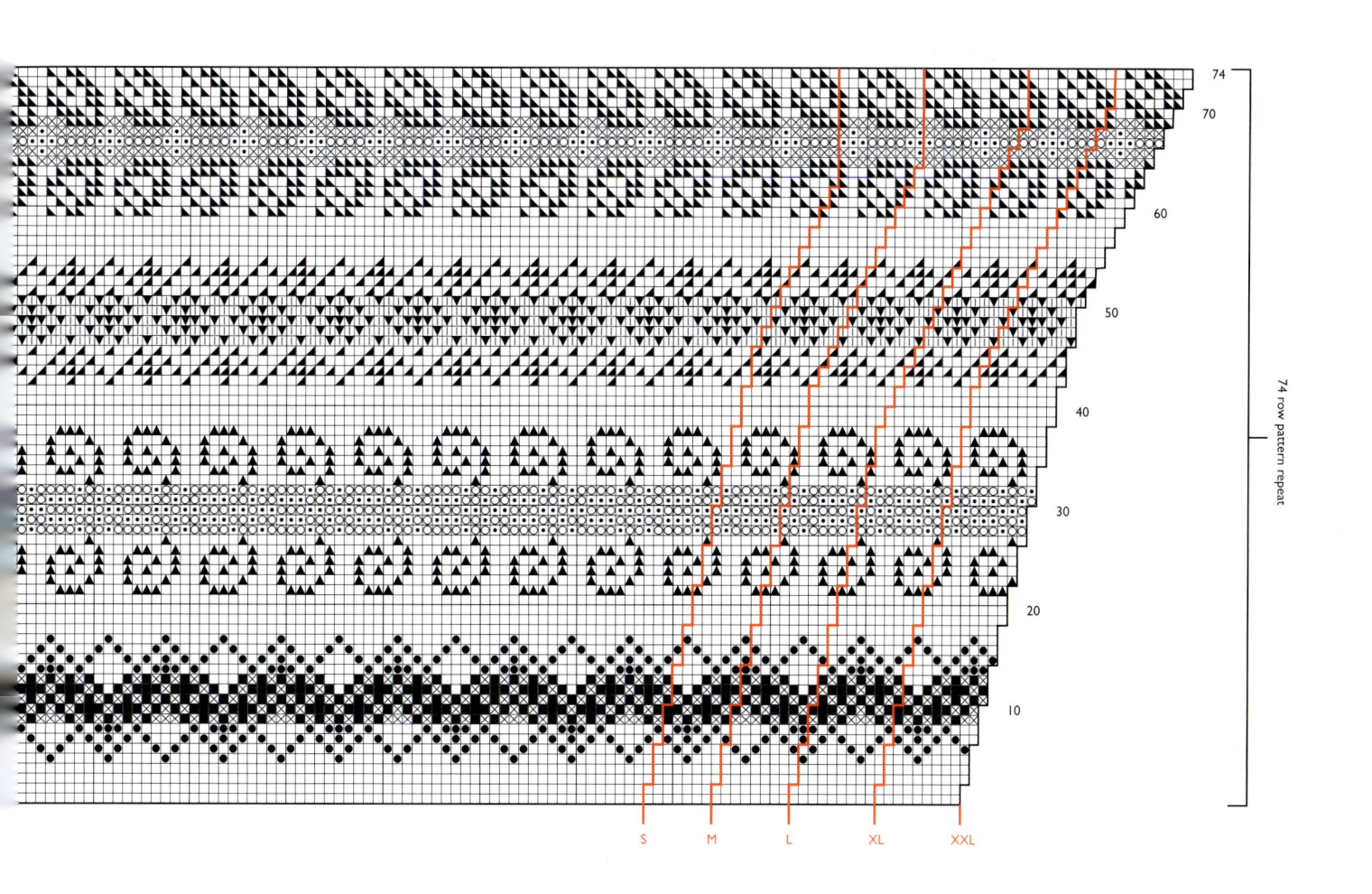

BIRCH

● ●

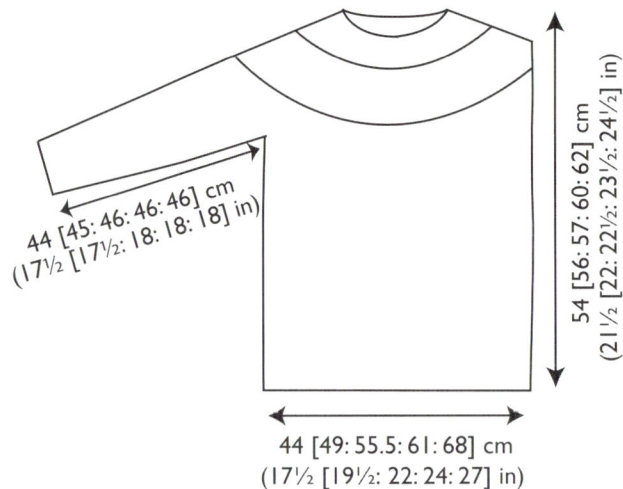

	S	M	L	XL	XXL	
To fit bust	81-86	91-97	102-107	112-117	122-127	cm
	32-34	36-38	40-42	44-46	48-50	in

Marie Wallin British Breeds

A Eau de Nil	12	14	16	17	20	x 25gm
B Woad	1	1	1	1	1	x 25gm
C Mulberry	1	1	1	1	1	x 25gm
D Wood	1	1	1	1	1	x 25gm
E Lime Flower	1	1	1	1	1	x 25gm
F Dark Apple	1	1	1	1	1	x 25gm
G Chestnut	1	1	1	1	1	x 25gm
H Raw	1	1	1	1	1	x 25gm

Needles

2¼mm (no 13) (US 1) circular needle
2¾mm (no 12) (US 2) circular needle
3¼mm (no 10) (US 3) circular needle
Set of 4 double-pointed 2¼mm (no 13) (US 1) needles
Set of 4 double-pointed 2¾mm (no 12) (US 2) needles
Set of 4 double-pointed 3¼mm (no 10) (US 3) needles

Tension

28 sts and 36 rounds to 10 cm measured over plain st st using 2¾mm (US 2) needles. 28 sts and 29 rounds to 10 cm measured over patterned st st using 3¼mm (US 3) needles.

BODY (knitted in one piece to armholes)
Using 2¼mm (US 1) circular needle and yarn A cast on 246 [274: 310: 342: 382] sts.
Taking care not to twist cast-on edge, work in rounds as folls:
Round 1 (RS): *K1, P1, rep from * to end.
This round forms rib.
Place marker on first st of round just knitted to denote beg and end of rounds – this marker denotes centre back st.
Work in rib for a further 25 rounds.
Change to 2¾mm (US 2) circular needle.
Now work in st st (K every round) until body meas 28 [29: 30: 31: 32] cm.
Divide for armholes
Next round: K marked centre back st and next 56 [63: 72: 80: 90] sts and slip these 57 [64: 73: 81: 91] sts onto a holder (for left back), K next 10 sts and slip these sts onto another holder (for left underarm), K next 113 [127: 145: 161: 181] sts and slip these sts onto another holder (for front), K next 10 sts and slip these sts onto another holder (for right underarm), K rem 56 [63: 72: 80: 90] sts and slip these sts onto another holder (for right back).
Break yarn.

SLEEVES

Using set of 4 double-pointed 2¼mm (US 1) needles and yarn A cast on 54 [56: 58: 58: 62] sts.
Taking care not to twist cast-on edge and placing marker between first and last sts of first round to denote beg and end

of rounds (this marker "sits" along sleeve "seam"), work in rib as given for body for 26 rounds.
Change to double-pointed 2¾mm (US 2) needles.
Now working in st st (K every round), cont as folls:
Work 4 [4: 4: 2: 2] rounds.
Next round (RS): K1, M1, K to last st, M1, K1. 56 [58: 60: 60: 64] sts.
Working all sleeve increases as set by last round, inc 1 st at each end of 6th [6th: 6th: 4th: 4th] and every foll 6th round to 82 [90: 88: 100: 104] sts, then on 4 [2: 4: 0: 0] foll 8th rounds. 90 [94: 96: 100: 104] sts.
Cont straight until sleeve meas 44 [45: 46: 46: 46] cm.
Next round: K5 and slip these sts onto a holder (for underarm), K to last 5 sts, K rem 5 sts and slip these 5 sts onto same holder as first 5 sts (so there are 10 sts on underarm holder).
Break yarn and leave rem 80 [84: 86: 90: 94] sts on another holder.

YOKE
With RS facing, using 2¾mm (US 2) circular needle and yarn A, work across all sts from holders as folls: K57 [64: 73: 81: 91] sts on left back holder, place marker on needle, K80 [84: 86: 90: 94] sts on left sleeve holder, place 2nd marker on needle,
K113 [127: 145: 161: 181] sts on front holder, place 3rd marker on needle, K80 [84: 86: 90: 94] sts on right sleeve holder, place 4th marker on needle, then K56 [63: 72: 80: 90] sts on right back holder. 386 [422: 462: 502: 550] sts.
There should be 4 markers on needle – each of these markers denotes a raglan armhole "seam". Place 5th marker on first st of round just worked to denote beg and end of rounds (this marker also denotes centre back st).
Working in st st throughout, cont as folls:
Next round (RS): *K to within 2 sts of "raglan" marker, K2tog, slip "raglan" marker onto right needle, sl 1, K1, psso, rep from * 3 times more, K to end. 378 [414: 454: 494: 542] sts.
Next round: Knit.
Rep last 2 rounds 15 [17: 18: 20: 22] times more, then first of these rounds (the dec round) again. 250 [270: 302: 326: 358] sts.

(**Note:** As number of sts decreases, change from circular needle to set of double-pointed needles).
Remove "raglan" markers but do NOT remove centre back marker.
Next round: K12 [11: 14: 27: 28], K2tog, (K7 [17: 19: 52: 58], K2tog) 25 [13: 13: 5: 5] times, K11 [10: 13: 27: 28].
224 [256: 288: 320: 352] sts.
Change to 3¼mm (US 3) circular needle.
Pattern note: when working the fairisle yoke, strand yarn a little more loosely than normal so as not to restrict the band when being worn.
Joining in and breaking off colours as required, using the **fairisle** technique as described on the information page and repeating the 32 st patt repeat 7 [8: 9: 10: 11] times around each round, work rounds 1 to 29 of chart, which is worked entirely in st st (K every round).
Change to 2¾mm (US 2) needle(s).
Now working in st st using yarn A only, complete yoke as folls:
Work 1 round.
Next round: K1 [21: 17: 9: 6], sl 1, K1, psso, (K2 [1: 1: 1: 1], sl 1, K1, psso) 55 [71: 84: 100: 113] times, K1 [20: 17: 9: 5].
168 [184: 203: 219: 238] sts.
Work 18 rounds.
Next round: K1 [20: 17: 9: 5], K2tog, (K1 [0: 0: 0: 0], K2tog) 55 [71: 84: 100: 113] times, K0 [20: 16: 8: 5].
112 [112: 118: 118: 124] sts.
Work neckband
Change to 2¼mm (US 1) needle(s).
Work in rib as given for body for 5 rounds.
Cast off **loosely** in rib.

MAKING UP
Press as described on the information page.
Join underarm seams by grafting together sets of 10 sts on underarm holders.
See information page for finishing instructions.

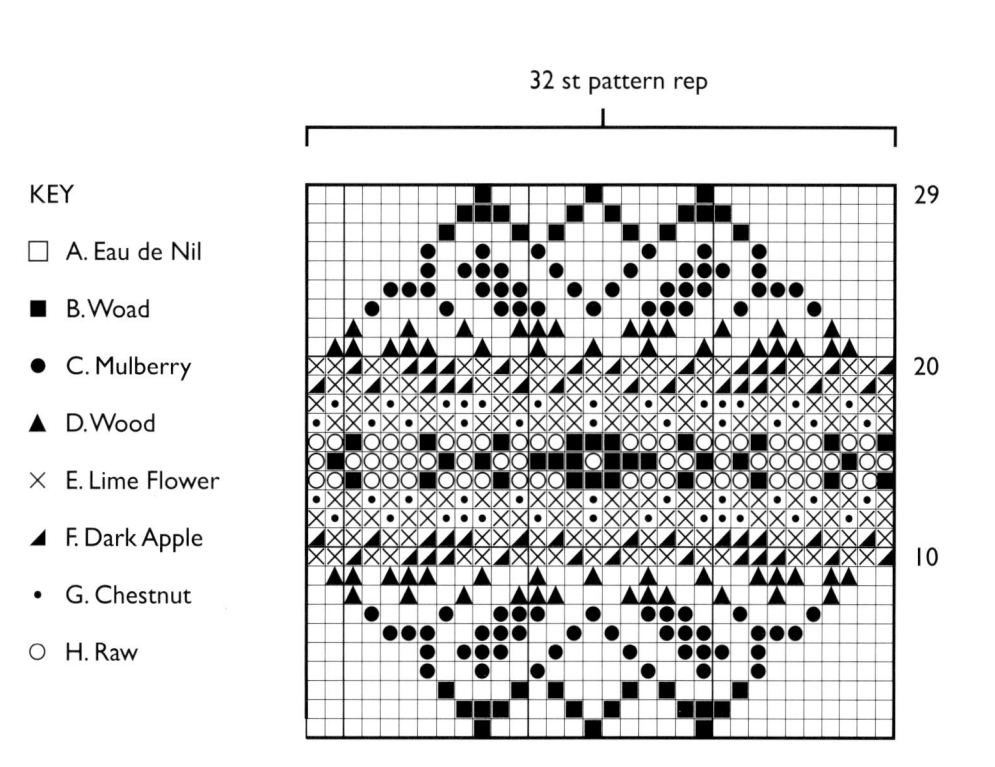

KEY
□ A. Eau de Nil
■ B. Woad
● C. Mulberry
▲ D. Wood
✕ E. Lime Flower
◢ F. Dark Apple
· G. Chestnut
○ H. Raw

MAPLE SCARF

Sizes
One size only

Marie Wallin British Breeds
A	Quince	3	x 25gm
B	Dark Apple	2	x 25gm
C	Wood	2	x 25gm
D	Russet	1	x 25gm
E	Raw	1	x 25gm
F	Lime Flower	2	x 25gm
G	Woad	2	x 25gm
H	Chestnut	1	x 25gm
I	Eau de Nil	2	x 25gm
J	Rose	1	x 25gm

Needles
3¼mm (no 10) (US 3) circular needle no more than 40 cm long

Tension
28 sts and 29 rounds to 10 cm measured over patterned st st using 3¼mm (US 3) circular needle.

Finished size
Completed scarf measures 19.5cm (7½ in) wide and 130cm (51 in) long.

SCARF
Using 3¼mm (US 3) circular needle and yarn A cast on 110 sts. Joining in and breaking off colours as required, using the **fairisle** technique as described on the information page and repeating the 22 st patt repeat 5 times around each round and repeating the 47 round patt repeat throughout, cont in patt from chart, which is worked entirely in st st (K every round), for 376 rounds (8 patt repeats).
Cast off.

FINISHING
Press as described on the information page.
Sew in any loose ends on WS of scarf.
Smooth out the scarf so that it is flat and close the bottom edges together and the top edges together using mattress stitch.

KEY

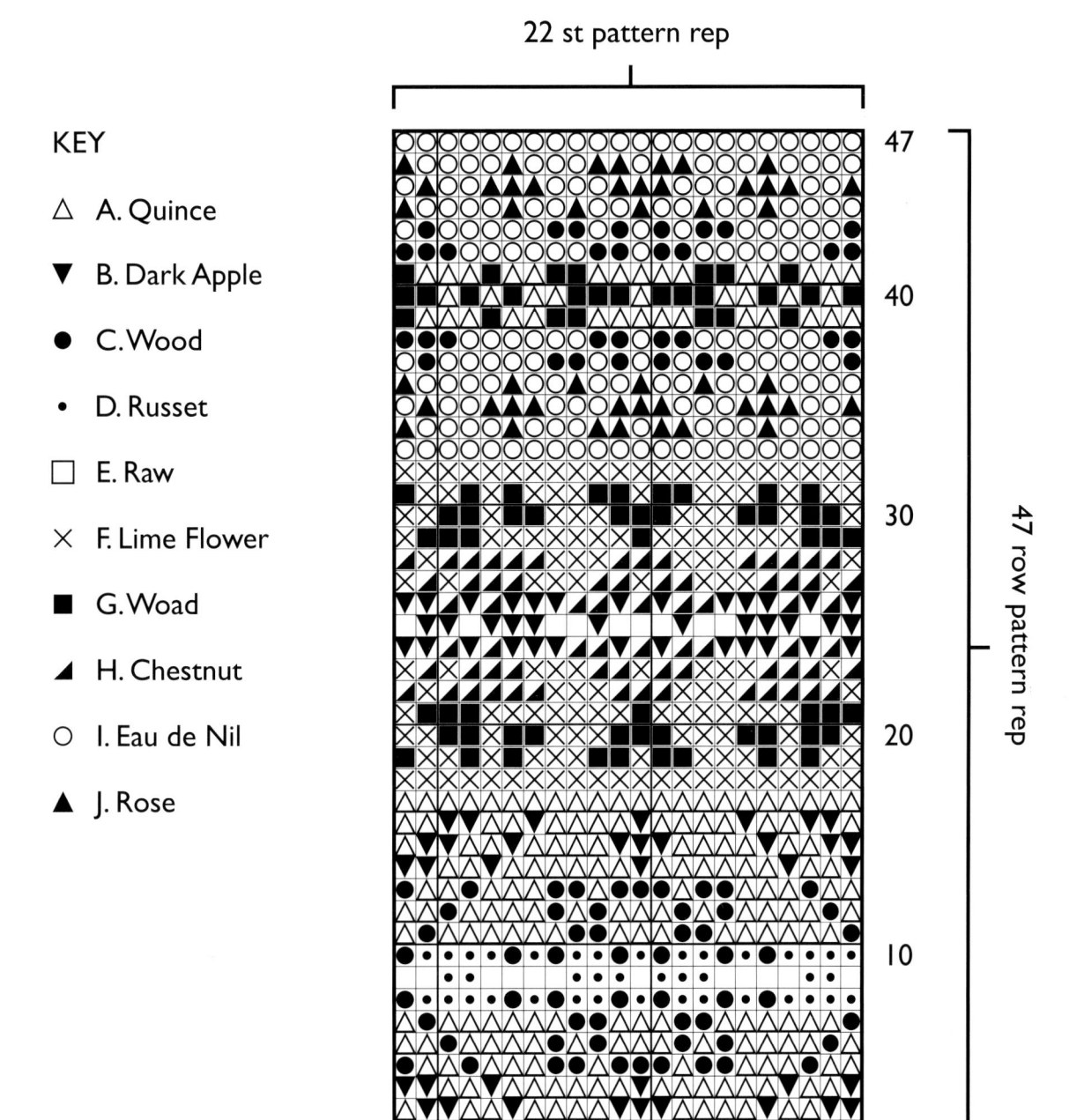

- △ A. Quince
- ▼ B. Dark Apple
- ● C. Wood
- · D. Russet
- □ E. Raw
- × F. Lime Flower
- ■ G. Woad
- ▲ H. Chestnut
- ○ I. Eau de Nil
- ▲ J. Rose

22 st pattern rep

47 row pattern rep

YEW

● ● ●

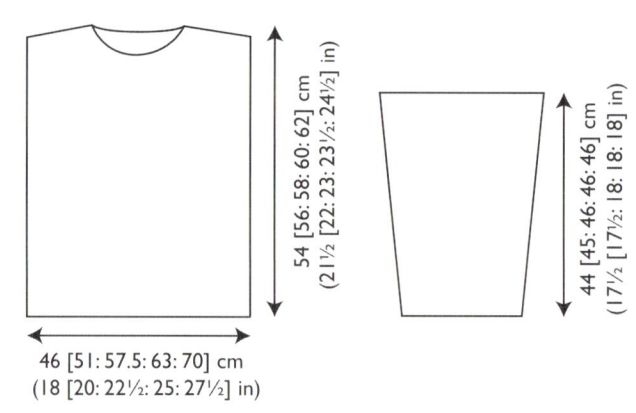

46 [51: 57.5: 63: 70] cm
(18 [20: 22½: 25: 27½] in)

54 [56: 58: 60: 62] cm
(21½ [22: 23: 23½: 24½] in)

44 [45: 46: 46: 46] cm
(17½ [17½: 18: 18: 18] in)

	S	M	L	XL	XXL	
To fit bust	81-86	91-97	102-107	112-117	122-127	cm
	32-34	36-38	40-42	44-46	48-50	in

Marie Wallin British Breeds
16   18   21   23   25   x 25gm
(photographed in Lime Flower)

Needles
1 pair 2¾mm (no 12) (US 2) needles
1 pair 3¼mm (no 10) (US 3) needles
Cable needle

Tension
28 sts and 36 rows to 10 cm measured over rev st st using 3¼mm (US 3) needles. Body panel (148 sts, dec to 146 sts) measures 43 cm, and sleeve panel (62 sts) measures 17 cm.

Special abbreviations
C4B = slip next 2 sts onto cable needle and leave at back of work, K2, then K2 from cable needle; **C4F** = slip next 2 sts onto cable needle and leave at front of work, K2, then K2 from cable needle; **Tw2L** = K into back of second st on left needle, K tog tbl first 2 sts on left needle and slip both sts off left needle together; **Tw2R** = K2tog leaving sts on left needle, K first st again and slip both sts off left needle together.

BACK
Using 2¾mm (US 2) needles cast on 156 [170: 188: 204: 224] sts.
Now work in patt, placing chart for body as folls:
Row 1 (WS): K0 [1: 0: 0: 0], (P1, K1) 2 [5: 10: 14: 19] times, work next 148 sts as row 1 of chart for body, (K1, P1) 2 [5: 10: 14: 19] times, K0 [1: 0: 0: 0].
Row 2: P0 [1: 0: 0: 0], (K1, P1) 2 [5: 10: 14: 19] times, work next 148 sts as row 2 of chart for body, (P1, K1) 2 [5: 10: 14: 19] times, P0 [1: 0: 0: 0].
These 2 rows set the sts – centre 148 sts worked in patt from chart for body with edge sts in rib.
Keeping sts correct as now set, cont as folls:
Work chart rows 3 and 4, then rep chart rows 1 to 4, 5 times more, ending with WS facing for next row. 24 rows worked in total.
Change to 3¼mm (US 3) needles.
Row 25 (WS): K4 [11: 20: 28: 38], work next 148 sts as row 5 of chart for body, K4 [11: 20: 28: 38].
Row 26: P4 [11: 20: 28: 38], work next 148 sts as row 6 of chart for body, P4 [11: 20: 28: 38].
These 2 rows set the sts for rest of back – centre 148 sts still in patt from chart for body with edge sts now in rev st st.
Keeping sts correct as now set, cont as folls:
Work chart rows 7 to 74. 154 [168: 186: 202: 222] sts.
Now repeating the 16, 20 and 24 row patt repeats as required and beg with chart row 75, cont in patt as now set as folls:
Cont straight until back meas 51 [53: 55: 57: 59] cm, ending with RS facing for next row.
Shape shoulders and back neck
Keeping patt correct, cast off 7 [9: 10: 11: 13] sts at beg of next 2 rows. 140 [150: 166: 180: 196] sts.

Next row (RS): Cast off 8 [9: 10: 11: 13] sts, patt until there are 38 [42: 48: 54: 59] sts on right needle and turn, leaving rem sts on a holder.

Work each side of neck separately.

Dec 1 st at neck edge of next 6 rows **and at same time** cast off 8 [9: 10: 12: 13] sts at beg of 2nd and foll alt row, then 8 [9: 11: 12: 13] sts at beg of foll alt row.

Work 1 row.

Cast off rem 8 [9: 11: 12: 14] sts.

With RS facing, slip centre 48 [48: 50: 50: 52] sts onto a holder (for neckband), rejoin yarn and patt to end.

Complete to match first side, reversing shapings.

FRONT

Work as given for back until 12 [12: 14: 14: 16] rows less have been worked than on back to beg of shoulder shaping, ending with RS facing for next row.

Shape front neck

Next row (RS): Patt 60 [67: 76: 84: 94] sts and turn, leaving rem sts on a holder.

Work each side of neck separately.

Keeping patt correct, dec 1 st at neck edge of next 8 rows, then on foll 1 [1: 2: 2: 3] alt rows. 51 [58: 66: 74: 83] sts.

Work 1 row, ending with RS facing for next row.

Shape shoulder

Keeping patt correct, cast off 7 [9: 10: 11: 13] sts at beg of next and foll 0 [4: 3: 1: 4] alt rows, then 8 [-: 11: 12: -] sts at beg of foll 4 [-: 1: 3: -] alt rows **and at same time** dec 1 st at neck edge of next and foll 3 alt rows.

Work 1 row.

Cast off rem 8 [9: 11: 12: 14] sts.

With RS facing, slip centre 34 sts onto a holder (for neckband), rejoin yarn and patt to end.

Complete to match first side, reversing shapings.

SLEEVES

Using 2¾mm (US 2) needles cast on 68 [70: 74: 74: 76] sts.

Now work in patt, placing chart for sleeve as folls:

Row 1 (WS): K1 [0: 0: 0: 1], (P1, K1) 1 [2: 3: 3: 3] times, work next 62 sts as row 1 of chart for sleeve, (K1, P1) 1 [2: 3: 3: 3] times, K1 [0: 0: 0: 1].

Row 2: P1 [0: 0: 0: 1], (K1, P1) 1 [2: 3: 3: 3] times, work next 62 sts as row 2 of chart for sleeve, (P1, K1) 1 [2: 3: 3: 3] times, P1 [0: 0: 0: 1].

These 2 rows set the sts – centre 62 sts worked in patt from chart for sleeve with edge sts in rib.

Keeping sts correct as now set, cont as folls:

Work chart rows 3 and 4, then rep chart rows 1 to 4, 5 times more, ending with **WS** facing for next row. 24 rows worked in total.

Change to 3¼mm (US 3) needles.

Row 25 (WS): K3 [4: 6: 6: 7], work next 62 sts as row 5 of chart for sleeve, K3 [4: 6: 6: 7].

Row 26: P3 [4: 6: 6: 7], work next 62 sts as row 6 of chart for sleeve, P3 [4: 6: 6: 7].

SLEEVE CHART

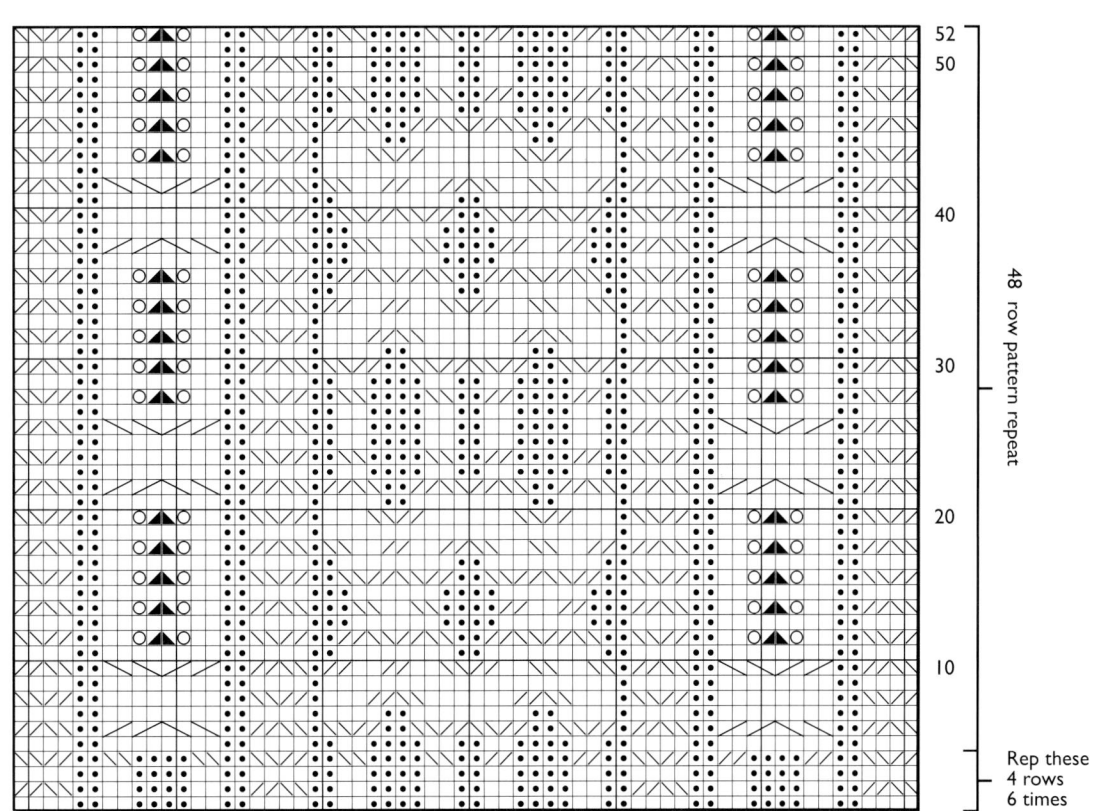

BODY CHART
KEY

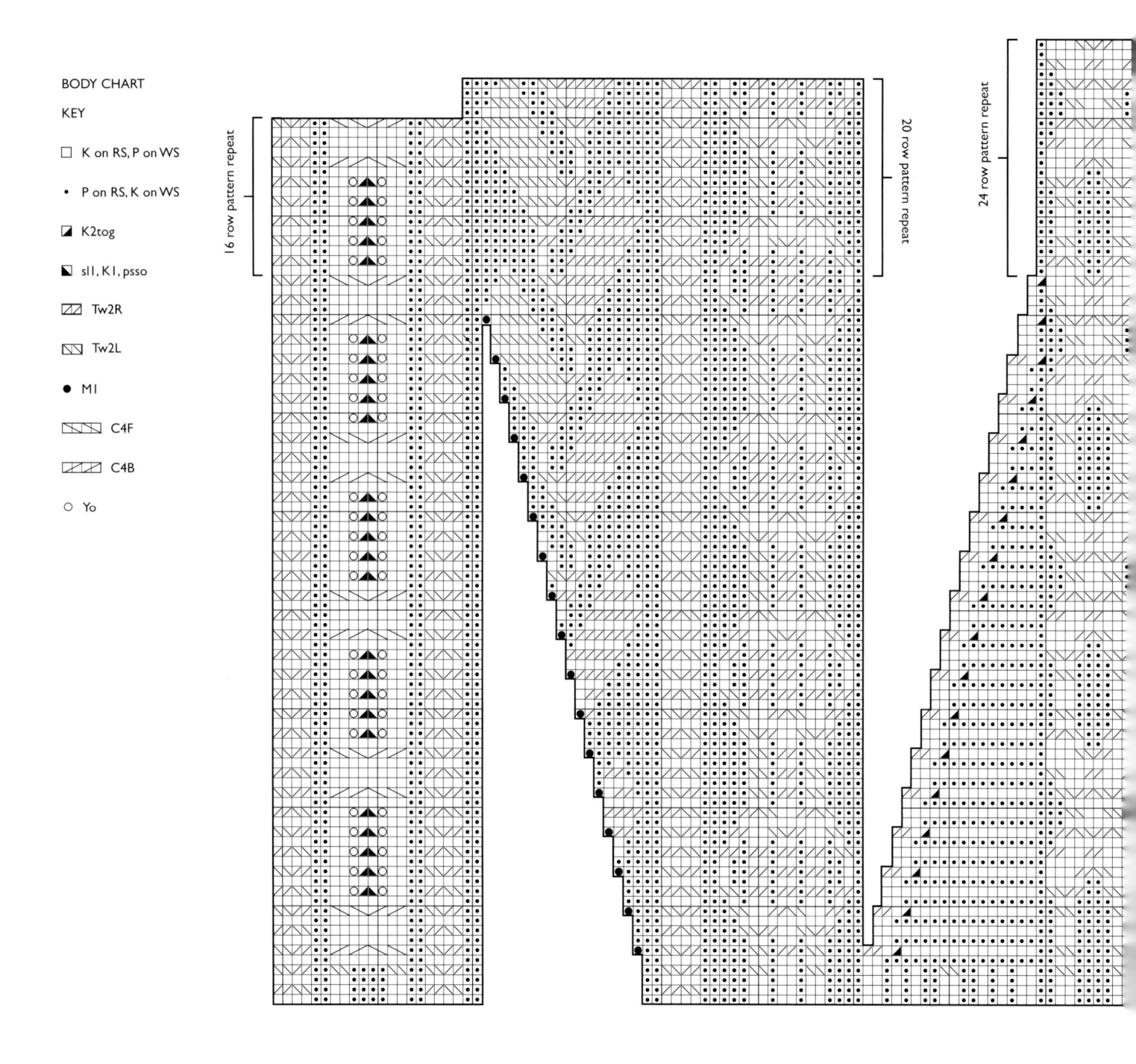

□ K on RS, P on WS

• P on RS, K on WS

◢ K2tog

◣ sl1, K1, psso

▨ Tw2R

▧ Tw2L

• M1

▨▨ C4F

▧▧ C4B

○ Yo

16 row pattern repeat

20 row pattern repeat

24 row pattern repeat

These 2 rows set the sts for rest of sleeve – centre 62 sts still in patt from chart for sleeve with edge sts now in rev st st.
Keeping sts correct as now set and repeating the 48 row patt repeat throughout, cont as folls:
Inc 1 st at each end of 4th [2nd: 2nd: 2nd: 2nd] and every foll 6th [6th: 4th: 4th: 4th] row to 96 [110: 78: 90: 104] sts, then on every foll 8th [-: 6th: 6th: 6th] row until there are 104 [-: 116: 120: 126] sts, taking inc sts into rev st st.
Cont straight until sleeve meas 44 [45: 46: 46: 46] cm, ending with RS facing for next row.
Cast off.

MAKING UP
Press as described on the information page.
Join right shoulder seam using back stitch, or mattress stitch if preferred.
Neckband
With RS facing and using 2¾mm (US 2) needles, pick up and knit

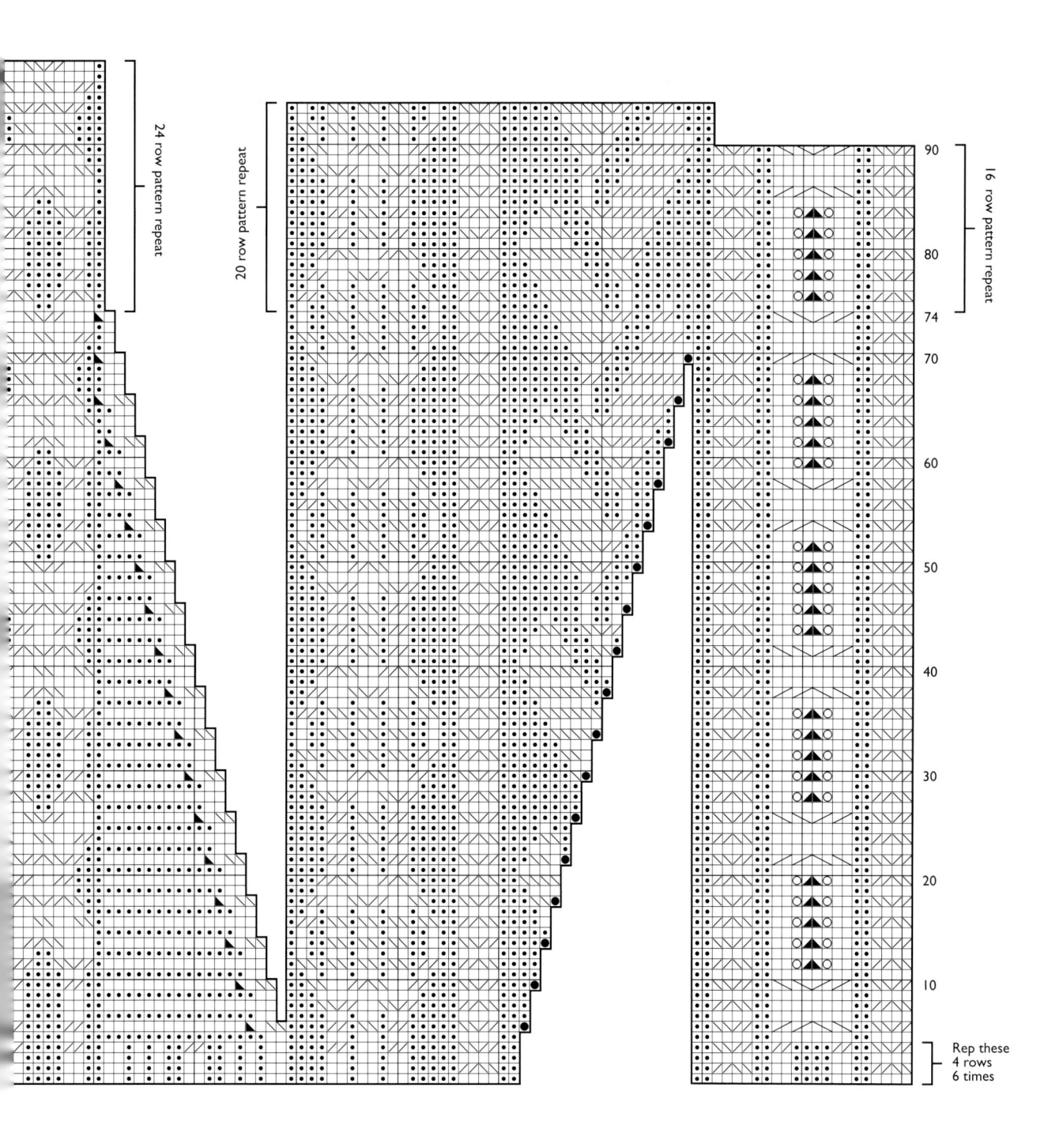

22 [22: 24: 24: 26] sts down left side of front neck, K across 34 sts on front holder dec 1 st at centre, pick up and knit 22 [22: 24: 24: 26] sts up right side of front neck, and 7 sts down right side of back neck, K across 48 [48: 50: 50: 52] sts on back holder, then pick up and knit 7 sts up left side of back neck. 139 [139: 145: 145: 151] sts.
Row 1 (WS): K1, *P1, K1, rep from * to end.
Row 2: P1, *K1, P1, rep from * to end.
These 2 rows form rib.

Cont in rib for a further 3 rows, ending with RS facing for next row.
Cast off in rib.
Join left shoulder and neckband seam. Mark points along side seam edges 17 [18: 19: 20: 21] cm either side of shoulder seams, then sew cast-off edge of sleeves to back and front between these points. Join side and sleeve seams.
See information page for finishing instructions.

ROWAN COWL

Sizes

One size only

Marie Wallin British Breeds

A	Eau de Nil	1	x 25gm
B	Raw	1	x 25gm
C	Chestnut	1	x 25gm
D	Lime Flower	1	x 25gm
E	Russet	1	x 25gm
F	Quince	1	x 25gm
G	Rose	1	x 25gm
H	Woad	1	x 25gm
I	Wood	1	x 25gm
J	Dark Apple	1	x 25gm
K	Mallard	1	x 25gm

Needles

2¾mm (no 12) (US 2) circular needle
3¼mm (no 10) (US 3) circular needle

Tension

28 sts and 29 rounds to 10 cm measured over patterned st st using 3¼mm (US 3) circular needle.

Finished size

Completed cowl measures 78.5 cm (31 in) wide (in total all round) and 22 cm (8½ in) deep.

COWL

Bottom welt
Using 2¾mm (US 2) circular needle and yarn K cast on 220 sts.
Taking care not to twist cast-on edge, work in rounds as folls:
Round 1 (RS): *K1, P1; rep from * to end.
This round forms rib.
Place marker on first st of round just knitted to denote beg and end of rounds.
Cont in rib for a further 6 rounds.
Next round: Purl.
Next round: Knit.
Break off yarn K.
Change to 3¼mm (US 3) circular needle.
Joining in and breaking off colours as required, using the **fairisle** technique as described on the information page and repeating the 20 st patt repeat 11 times around each round, work rounds 1 to 51 of chart, which is worked entirely in st st (K every round).
Break off yarns.
Top welt
Change to 2¾mm (US 2) circular needle and join in yarn K.
Next round: Knit.
Next round: Purl.
Work 7 rounds in rib as given for bottom welt.
Cast off in rib.

FINISHING

Press as described on the information page.
Sew in any loose ends on WS of cowl.

KEY

- ○ A. Eau de Nil
- □ B. Raw
- ◣ C. Chestnut
- ✕ D. Lime Flower
- • E. Russet
- △ F. Quince
- ■ G. Rose
- ▲ H. Woad
- ● I. Wood
- ▼ J. Dark Apple

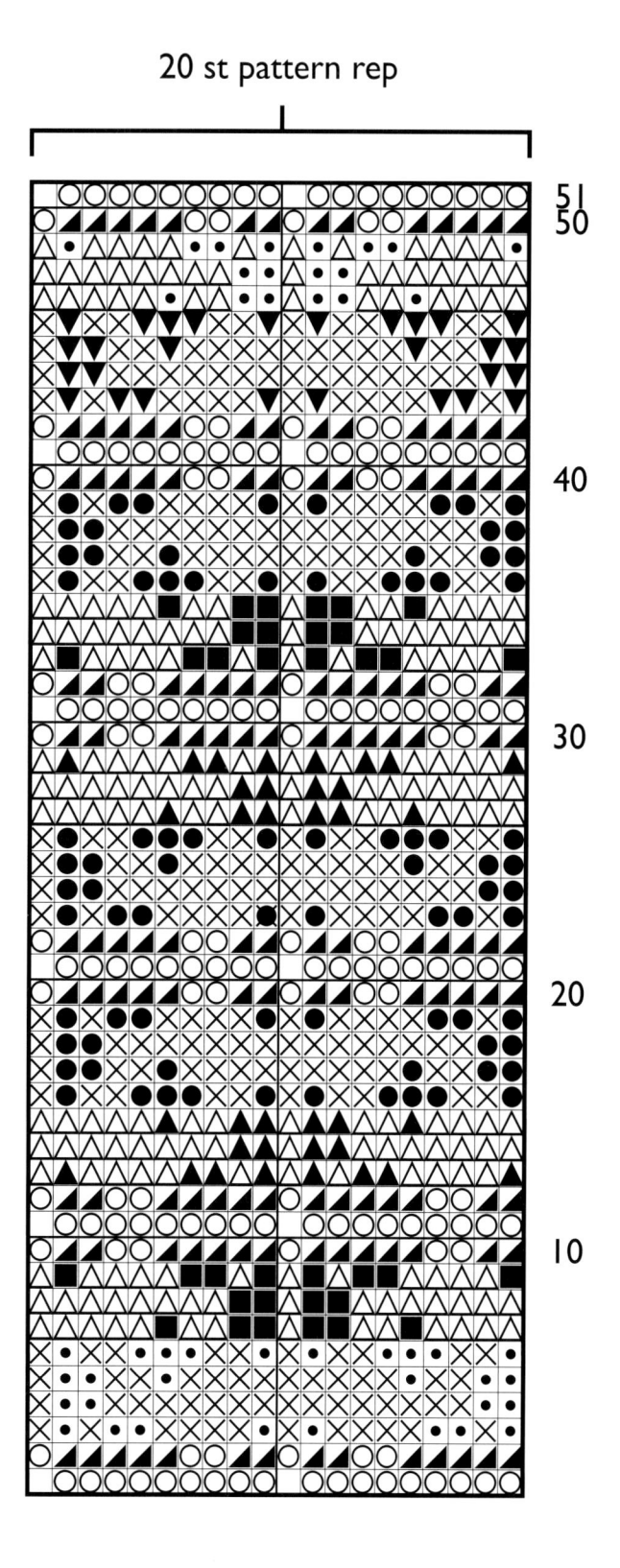

20 st pattern rep

WALNUT TAM

One size only
To fit average head
53 – 56cm (21 – 22in)

Marie Wallin British Breeds

A	Mallard	1	x 25gm
B	Quince	1	x 25gm
C	Dark Apple	1	x 25gm
D	Eau de Nil	1	x 25gm
E	Wood	1	x 25gm
F	Raw	1	x 25gm
G	Russet	1	x 25gm
H	Mulberry	1	x 25gm
I	Rose	1	x 25gm
J	Chestnut	1	x 25gm

Needles
2¾mm (no 12) (US 2) circular needle or set of 4 double-pointed
2¾mm (no 12) (US 2) needles
3¼mm (no 10) (US 3) circular needle or set of 4 double-pointed
3¼mm (no 10) (US 3) needles

Tension
28 sts and 29 rounds to 10 cm measured over patterned st st using 3¼mm (US 3) needles.

TAM
Brim
Using 2¾mm (US 2) circular needle or double-pointed needles and yarn F cast on 114 sts.
Taking care not to twist cast-on edge, work in rounds as folls:
Round 1 (RS): *K1, P1, rep from * to end.
Place marker on first st of round just knitted to denote beg and end of rounds.
Join in yarn I.
Keeping yarn not in use at **WS** of work, cont as folls:
Round 2: *Using yarn F K1, using yarn I P1, rep from * to end.
Rep round 2, 3 times more, Break off yarn I and cont in yarn F **only**.
Next round: *K1, P1, rep from * to end.
Next round: K2tog, K to last 2 sts, K2tog. 112 sts.
Break off yarn F.
Change to 3¼mm (US 3) circular needle or double-pointed needles.
Join in yarn A.
Increase round: Using yarn A, K1, *M1, K2, rep from * to last st, M1, K1. 168 sts.
Work sides and crown of tam
Joining in and breaking off colours as required and using the **fairisle** technique as described on the information page, work from chart, which is worked entirely in st st (K every round) as folls:
Beg with **round 2** of chart, work the first 12 sts of chart, rep the 24 st patt repeat 6 times, then work the last 12 sts of chart on each

round until round 62 has been completed, working decreases as indicated on the following rounds:
Round 41: (Patt 10 sts, sl 1, K2tog, psso, patt 11 sts) 7 times. 154 sts.
Round 43: (Patt 9 sts, sl 1, K2tog, psso, patt 10 sts) 7 times. 140 sts.
Round 45: (Patt 8 sts, sl 1, K2tog, psso, patt 9 sts) 7 times. 126 sts.
Round 47: (Patt 7 sts, sl 1, K2tog, psso, patt 8 sts) 7 times. 112 sts.
Round 49: (Patt 6 sts, sl 1, K2tog, psso, patt 7 sts) 7 times. 98 sts.
Round 51: (Patt 5 sts, sl 1, K2tog, psso, patt 6 sts) 7 times. 84 sts.
Round 53: (Patt 4 sts, sl 1, K2tog, psso, patt 5 sts) 7 times. 70 sts.
Round 55: (Patt 3 sts, sl 1, K2tog, psso, patt 4 sts) 7 times. 56 sts.
Round 57: (Patt 2 sts, sl 1, K2tog, psso, patt 3 sts) 7 times. 42 sts.
Round 59: (Patt 1 st, sl 1, K2tog, psso, patt 2 sts) 7 times. 28 sts.
Round 61: (Patt 1 st, sl 1, K2tog, psso) 7 times. 14 sts.
Round 62: Using yarn F, (K2tog) 7 times. 7 sts.
Break off yarn, thread through rem sts and draw up tightly.

FINISHING
Fasten off centre of tam on WS.
Weave in any loose ends on WS of tam.
Press tam gently on WS using a warm iron over a damp cloth.

KEY

⋀ A. Mallard

△ B. Quince

▼ C. Dark Apple

○ D. Eau de Nil

● E. Wood

□ F. Raw

· G. Russet

■ H. Mulberry

▲ I. Rose

◢ J. Chestnut

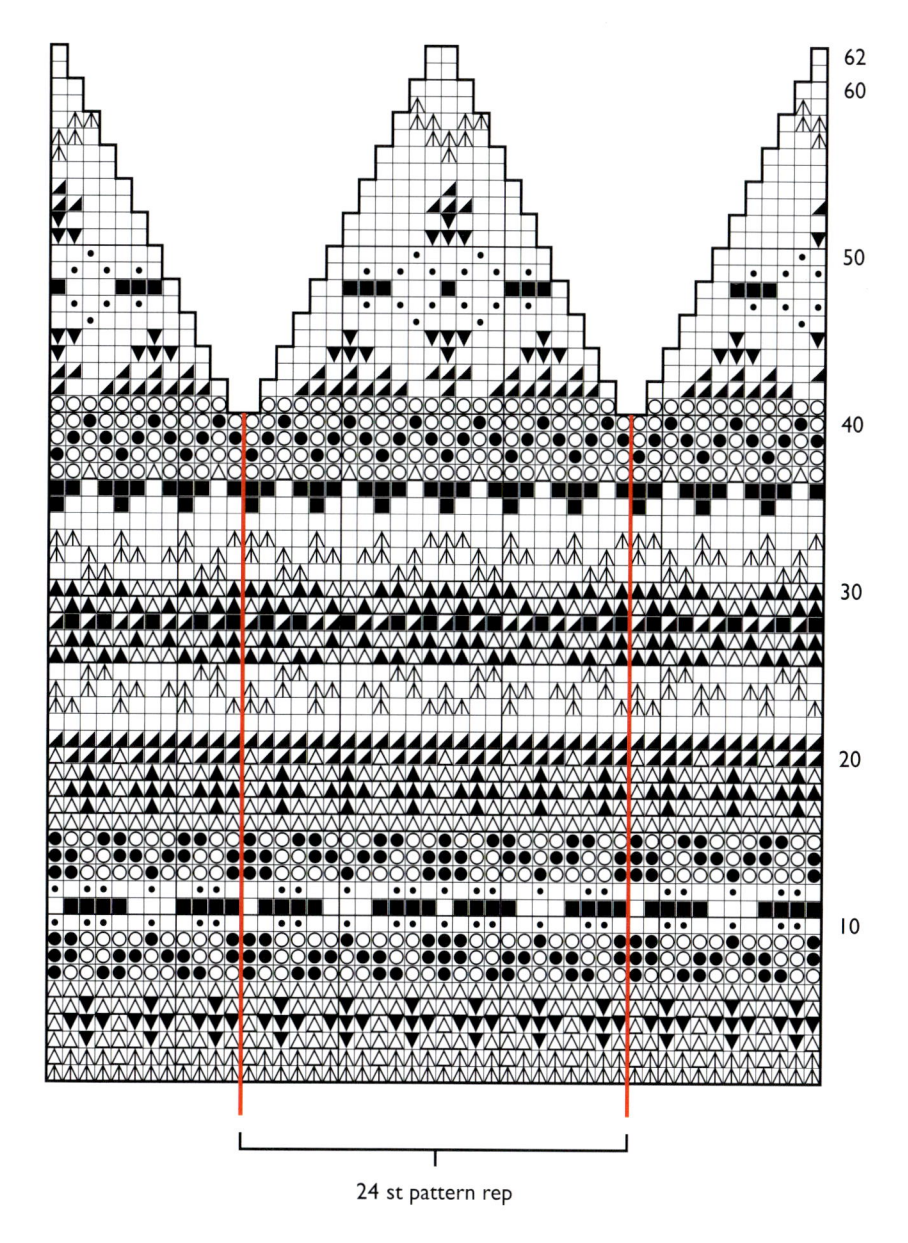

24 st pattern rep

SYCAMORE ARMWARMERS

Sizes
One size only

Marie Wallin British Breeds
A	Wood	1	x 25gm
B	Eau de Nil	1	x 25gm
C	Raw	1	x 25gm
D	Dark Apple	1	x 25gm
E	Russet	1	x 25gm
F	Quince	1	x 25gm
G	Mallard	1	x 25gm
H	Rose	1	x 25gm
I	Lime Flower	1	x 25gm
J	Chestnut	1	x 25gm

Note
Armwarmers can be knitted in rows on straight needles or in rounds on circular needles or double-pointed needles.

Needles

For armwarmers knitted in rows
1 pair 2¾mm (no 12) (US 2) needles
1 pair 3¼mm (no 10) (US 3) needles

For armwarmers knitted in rounds
2¾mm (no 12) (US 2) circular needle or set of 4 double-pointed 2¾mm (no 12) (US 2) needles
3¼mm (no 12) (US 3) circular needle or set of 4 double-pointed 3¼mm (no 10) (US 3) needles

Tension
28 sts and 29 rounds to 10 cm measured over patterned st st using 3¼mm (US 3) needles.

Finished size
Completed armwarmer measures 10.5 cm (4 in) wide and 24 cm (9½ in) long.

ARMWARMERS KNITTED IN ROWS

ARMWARMER (make 2)
Bottom welt
Using 2¾mm (US 2) needles and yarn C cast on 60 sts.
Row 1 (RS): *K2, P2, rep from * to end.
Join in yarn J.
Keeping yarn not in use at **WS** of work (this is back of work on RS rows, and front of work on WS rows), cont as folls:
Row 2: *Using yarn J K2, using yarn C P2, rep from * to end.
Row 3: *Using yarn C K2, using yarn J P2, rep from * to end.
Rep rows 2 and 3 twice more, ending with **WS** facing for next row.
Break off yarn J and cont in yarn C **only**.
Row 8 (WS): *K2, P2, rep from * to end.**
Break off yarn C.
Change to 3¼mm (US 3) needles.
Joining in and breaking off colours as required, using the **fairisle**

technique as described on the information page and repeating the 30 st patt repeat twice across each row, cont in patt from chart, which is worked entirely in st st beg with a K row, as folls:
Work chart rows 1 to 58, ending with RS facing for next row.
Break off yarns.
Top welt
Change to 2¾mm (US 2) needles and join in yarn C.
Work as given for bottom welt from ** to **.
Cast off in rib.

MAKING UP
Press as described on the information page.
Sew in any loose ends on WS of armwarmers.
Join side seam of armwarmers using mattress stitch.

ARMWARMERS KNITTED IN ROUNDS

ARMWARMER (make 2)
Bottom welt
Using 2¾mm (US 2) circular needle or double-pointed needles and yarn C cast on 60 sts.
Taking care not to twist cast-on edge, work in rounds as folls:
Round 1 (RS): *K2, P2, rep from * to end.
Place marker on first st of round just knitted to denote beg and end of rounds.
Join in yarn J.
Keeping yarn not in use at **WS** of work, cont as folls:
Round 2: *Using yarn C K2, using yarn J P2, rep from * to end.
Rep round 2, 5 times more.
Break off yarn J and cont in yarn C **only**.
Round 8: *K2, P2, rep from * to end.**
Break off yarn C.
Change to 3¼mm (US 3) circular needle or double-pointed needles.
Joining in and breaking off colours as required, using the **fairisle** technique as described on the information page and repeating the 30 st patt repeat twice around each round, cont in patt from chart, which is worked entirely in st st (K every round), as folls:
Work chart rounds 1 to 58.
Break off yarns.
Top welt
Change to 2¾mm (US 2) circular needles and join in yarn C.
Work as given for bottom welt from ** to **.
Cast off in rib.

FINISHING
Press as described on the information page.
Sew in any loose ends on WS of armwarmers.

KEY

■ A. Wood
× B. Eau de Nil
□ C. Raw
○ D. Dark Apple
△ E. Russet
• F. Quince
▲ G. Mallard
● H. Rose
╱ I. Lime Flower
◢ J. Chestnut

OAK

● ● ●

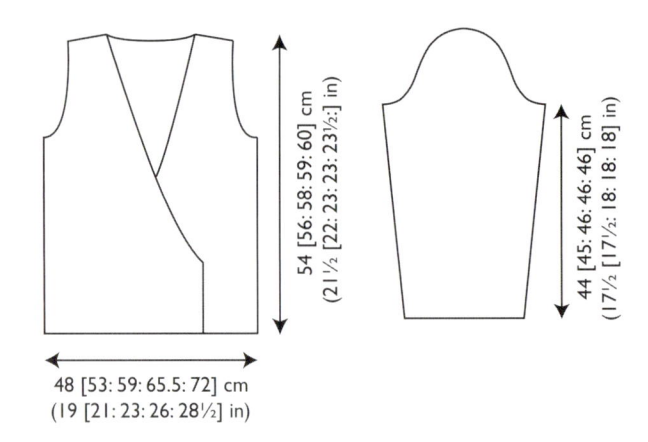

48 [53: 59: 65.5: 72] cm
(19 [21: 23: 26: 28½] in)

54 [56: 58: 59: 60] cm
(21½ [22: 23: 23: 23½] in)

44 [45: 46: 46: 46] cm
(17½ [17½: 18: 18: 18] in)

	S	M	L	XL	XXL	
To fit bust	81-86	91-97	102-107	112-117	122-127	cm
	32-34	36-38	40-42	44-46	48-50	in
Marie Wallin British Breeds
A Russet	2	2	3	3	3	x 25gm
B Lime Flower	3	3	4	4	4	x 25gm
C Chestnut	2	2	2	2	3	x 25gm
D Dark Apple	2	2	2	3	3	x 25gm
E Mallard	2	3	3	3	3	x 25gm
F Quince	2	2	2	2	3	x 25gm
G Raw	3	3	4	4	5	x 25gm
H Rose	1	1	1	1	1	x 25gm
I Wood	3	3	3	4	4	x 25gm
J Mulberry	1	1	1	1	2	x 25gm

Needles
1 pair 2¾mm (no 12) (US 2) needles
1 pair 3¼mm (no 10) (US 3) needles
2¾mm (no 12) (US 2) circular needle

Tension
28 sts and 29 rows to 10 cm measured over patterned st st using 3¼mm (US 3) needles.

BACK
Using 2¾mm (US 2) needles and yarn G cast on 135 [149: 165: 183: 201] sts.
Row 1 (RS): K1, *P1, K1, rep from * to end.

Join in yarn I.
Stranding yarn not in use across **WS** of work (this is front of work on WS rows, and back of work on RS rows), now work in 2 colour rib as folls:
Row 2 (WS): Using yarn G P1, *using yarn I K1, using yarn G P1, rep from * to end.
Row 3: Using yarn G K1, *using yarn I P1, using yarn G K1, rep from * to end.**
Rep last 2 rows twice more, then row 2 again, ending with RS facing for next row.
Break off yarn I and cont using yarn G **only**.
Row 9: As row 1.
Row 10: P1, *K1, P1, rep from * to end.
Change to 3¼mm (US 3) needles.
Beg and ending rows as indicated, using the **fairisle** technique as described on the information page and repeating the 84 row patt repeat throughout, cont in patt from chart, which is worked entirely in st st beg with a K row, as folls:
Work 88 [90: 92: 92: 92] rows, ending after chart row 4 [6: 8: 8: 8] and with RS facing for next row. (Back should meas approx 33 [34: 35: 35: 35] cm.)
Shape armholes
Keeping patt correct, cast off 6 [7: 8: 9: 10] sts at beg of next 2 rows. 123 [135: 149: 165: 181] sts.
Dec 1 st at each end of next 5 [7: 9: 11: 13] rows, then on foll 6 [7: 8: 10: 11] alt rows. 101 [107: 115: 123: 133] sts.
Cont straight until armhole meas 17 [18: 19: 20: 21] cm, ending with RS facing for next row.

Shape shoulders and back neck
Keeping patt correct, cast off 4 [4: 4: 5: 6] sts at beg of next 6 [6: 2: 6: 6] rows, then – [-: -: 5: -: -] sts at beg of foll – [-: -: 4: -: -] rows. 77 [83: 87: 93: 97] sts.
Next row (RS): Cast off 4 [4: 5: 5: 6] sts, patt until there are 16 [19: 19: 22: 22] sts on right needle and turn, leaving rem sts on a holder.
Work each side of neck separately.
Dec 1 st at neck edge of next 4 rows **and at same time** cast off 4 [5: 5: 6: 6] sts at beg of 2nd and foll alt row.
Work 1 row.
Cast off rem 4 [5: 5: 6: 6] sts.
With RS facing, slip centre 37 [37: 39: 39: 41] sts onto a holder (for front band), rejoin yarns and patt to end.
Complete to match first side, reversing shapings.

LEFT FRONT
Using 2¾mm (US 2) needles and yarn G cast on 96 [102: 110: 120: 128] sts.
Row 1 (RS): K1, *P1, K1, rep from * to last st, K1.
Join in yarn I.
Stranding yarn not in use across **WS** of work (this is front of work on WS rows, and back of work on RS rows), now work in 2 colour rib as folls:
Row 2 (WS): Using yarn G K1, P1, *using yarn I K1, using yarn G P1, rep from * to end.
Row 3: Using yarn G K1, *using yarn I P1, using yarn G K1, rep from * to last st, using G K1.
Rep last 2 rows twice more, then row 2 again, ending with RS facing for next row.
Break off yarn I and cont using yarn G **only**.
Row 9: As row 1.
Row 10: *K1, P1, rep from * to last 0 [2: 2: 0: 2] sts, (K1, inc in last st) 0 [1: 1: 0: 1] times. 96 [103: 111: 120: 129] sts.
Change to 3¼mm (US 3) needles.
Beg and ending rows as indicated, cont in patt from chart as folls:
Work 38 rows, ending with RS facing for next row.
Shape front slope
Keeping patt correct, dec 1 st at end of next row **and at same edge** on foll 10 [6: 2: 0: 0] rows, then on foll 19 [22: 25: 26: 26] alt rows. 66 [74: 83: 93: 102] sts.
Work 1 row, ending after chart row 4 [6: 8: 8: 8] and with RS facing for next row.
Shape armhole
Keeping patt correct, cast off 6 [7: 8: 9: 10] sts at beg and dec 1 st at end of next row. 59 [66: 74: 83: 91] sts.
Work 1 row.
Dec 1 st at armhole edge of next 5 [7: 9: 11: 13] rows, then on foll 6 [7: 8: 10: 11] alt rows **and at same time** dec 1 st at front slope edge of next and foll 8 [10: 12: 15: 17] alt rows.
39 [41: 44: 46: 49] sts.
Dec 1 st at front slope edge **only** on 2nd and foll 9 [8: 8: 6: 5] alt rows, then on foll 4th row. 28 [31: 34: 38: 42] sts.
Cont straight until left front matches back to beg of shoulder shaping, ending with RS facing for next row.
Shape shoulder
Keeping patt correct, cast off 4 [4: 4: 5: 6] sts at beg of next and foll 5 [3: 0: 3: 5] alt rows, then – [5: 5: 6: –] sts at beg of foll – [2: 5: 2: –] alt rows.
Work 1 row.
Cast off rem 4 [5: 5: 6: 6] sts.

RIGHT FRONT
Using 2¾mm (US 2) needles and yarn G cast on 96 [102: 110: 120: 128] sts.
Row 1 (RS): K2, *P1, K1, rep from * to end.
Join in yarn I.
Stranding yarn not in use across **WS** of work (this is front of work on WS rows, and back of work on RS rows), now work in 2 colour rib as folls:
Row 2 (WS): Using yarn G P1, *using yarn I K1, using yarn G P1, rep from * to last st, using yarn G K1.
Row 3: Using yarn G K2, *using yarn I P1, using yarn G K1, rep from * to end.
Rep last 2 rows twice more, then row 2 again, ending with RS facing for next row.
Break off yarn I and cont using yarn G **only**.
Row 9: As row 1.
Row 10: (Inc in first st, K1) 0 [1: 1: 0: 1] times, *P1, K1, rep from * to end. 96 [103: 111: 120: 129] sts.
Change to 3¼mm (US 3) needles.
Beg and ending rows as indicated, cont in patt from chart as folls:
Work 38 rows, ending with RS facing for next row.
Shape front slope
Keeping patt correct, dec 1 st at beg of next row **and at same edge** on foll 10 [6: 2: 0: 0] rows, then on foll 19 [22: 25: 26: 26] alt rows. 66 [74: 83: 93: 102] sts.
Complete to match left front, reversing shapings.

SLEEVES
Using 2¾mm (US 2) needles and yarn G cast on 53 [57: 59: 59: 61] sts.
Work from ** to ** as given for back.
Rep last 2 rows 3 times more, then row 2 again, ending with RS facing for next row.
Break off yarn I and cont using yarn G **only**.
Row 9 (RS): K2, *P1, K1, rep from * to end.
Row 10: *P1, K1, rep from * to last 2 sts, P2.
Change to 3¼mm (US 3) needles.
Beg and ending rows as indicated and **beg with chart row 57**, cont in patt from chart, as folls:
Inc 1 st at each end of 3rd and every foll 4th row to 75 [75: 81: 93: 101] sts, then on every foll 6th row until there are 95 [99: 103: 107: 111] sts, taking inc sts into patt.
Cont straight until sleeve meas approx 44 [45: 46: 46: 46] cm, ending after same chart row as on back to beg of armhole shaping and with RS facing for next row.
Shape top
Keeping patt correct, cast off 6 [7: 8: 9: 10] sts at beg of next 2 rows. 83 [85: 87: 89: 91] sts.
Dec 1 st at each end of next 9 rows, then on every foll alt row until 57 sts rem, then on foll 13 rows, ending with RS facing for next row. 31 sts.
Cast off 5 sts at beg of next 2 rows.
Cast off rem 21 sts.

MAKING UP
Press as described on the information page.
Join both shoulder seams using back stitch, or mattress stitch if preferred.
Front band
With RS facing, using 2¾mm (US 2) circular needle and yarn G, beg and ending at front cast-on edges, pick up and knit 49 sts up right front opening edge to beg of front slope shaping, 129 [132: 135: 138: 141] sts up right front slope to shoulder, and 5 sts down right side of back neck, K across 37 [37: 39: 39: 41] sts on back holder, pick up and knit 5 sts up left side of back neck, 129 [132: 135: 138: 141] sts down left front slope to beg of front

KEY

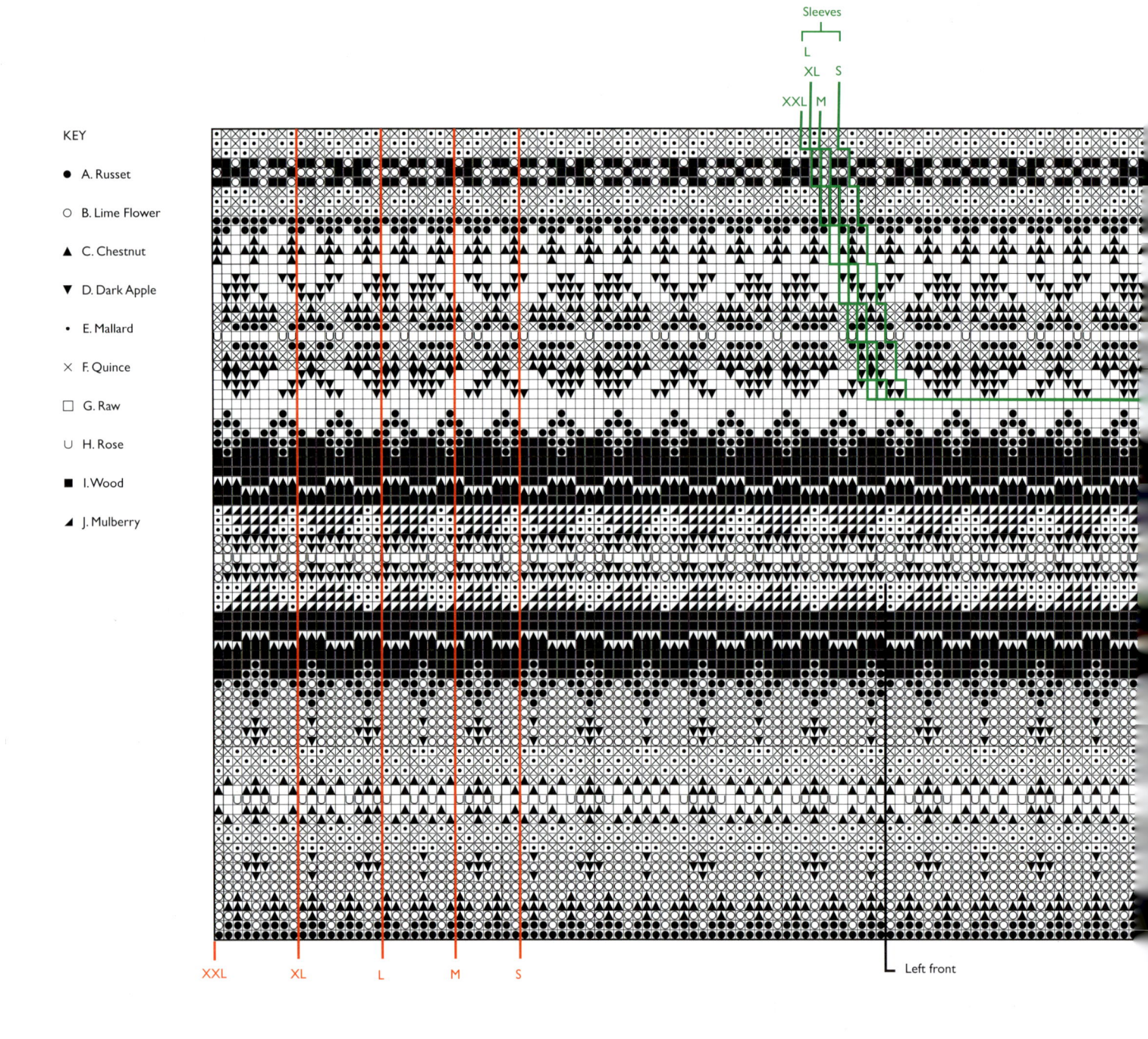

- ● A. Russet
- ○ B. Lime Flower
- ▲ C. Chestnut
- ▼ D. Dark Apple
- · E. Mallard
- × F. Quince
- □ G. Raw
- ∪ H. Rose
- ■ I. Wood
- ◢ J. Mulberry

slope shaping, and 49 sts down left front opening edge.
403 [409: 417: 423: 431] sts.
Join in yarn I.
Stranding yarn not in use across **WS** of work (this is front of work on WS rows, and back of work on RS rows), now work in 2 colour rib as folls:
Row 1 (WS): Using yarn G K1, P1, *using yarn I K1, using yarn G P1, rep from * to last st, using yarn G K1.

Row 2: Using yarn G K2, *using yarn I P1, using yarn G K1, rep from * to last st, using yarn G K1.
These 2 rows form 2 colour rib.
Cont in 2 colour rib for a further 3 rows, ending with RS facing for next row.
Using yarn G, cast off in rib.
Join side seams. Join sleeve seams. Insert sleeves into armholes.

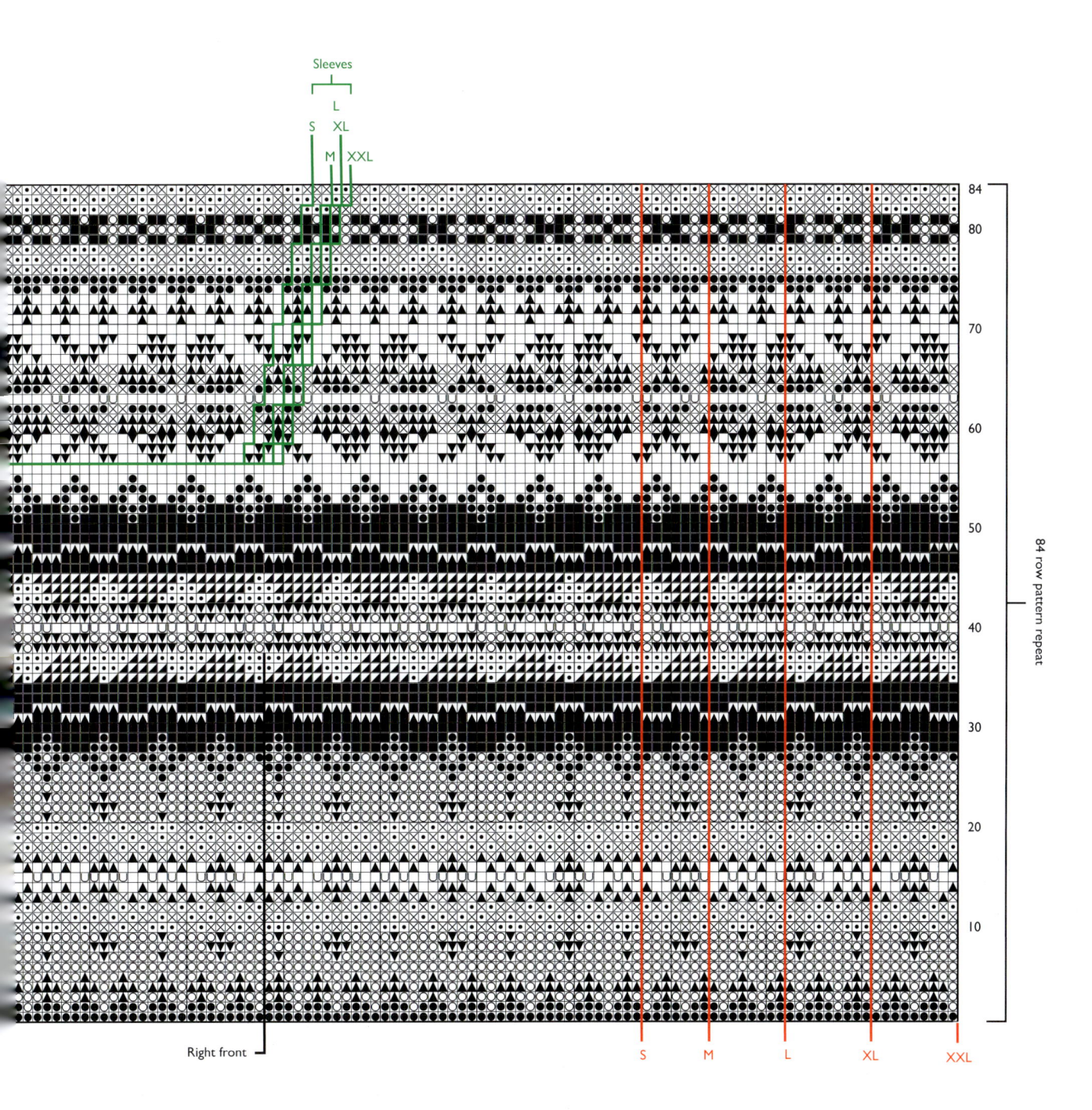

Sleeves

S M L XL XXL (sleeve size markers)

Right front

S M L XL XXL (body size markers)

84 row pattern repeat

CHESTNUT ●●●

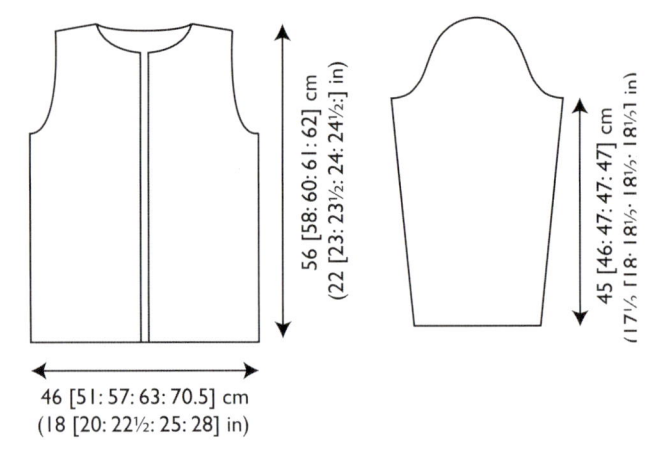

	S	M	L	XL	XXL	
To fit bust	81-86	91-97	102-107	112-117	122-127	cm
	32-34	36-38	40-42	44-46	48-50	in

Marie Wallin British Breeds

A	Raw	4	5	5	6	6	x 25gm
B	Wood	3	3	4	4	4	x 25gm
C	Russet	3	3	3	4	4	x 25gm
D	Quince	2	2	2	2	2	x 25gm
E	Eau de Nil	1	2	2	2	2	x 25gm
F	Lime Flower	2	2	2	2	3	x 25gm
G	Chestnut	2	2	2	2	2	x 25gm
H	Dark Apple	3	3	3	4	4	x 25gm

Needles
1 pair 2¾mm (no 12) (US 2) needles
1 pair 3¼mm (no 10) (US 3) needles

Buttons – 9 x TGB2741 14mm from Textile Garden, see information page for contact details.

Tension
28 sts and 29 rows to 10 cm measured over patterned st st using 3¼mm (US 3) needles.

BACK
Using 2¾mm (US 2) needles and yarn A cast on 129 [143: 159: 177: 197] sts.
Row 1 (RS): K1, *P1, K1, rep from * to end.

Joining in and breaking off colours as required and stranding yarn not in use across **WS** of work (this is front of work on WS rows, and back of work on RS rows), now work in striped 2 colour rib as folls:
Row 2 (WS): Using yarn A P1, *using yarn B K1, using yarn A P1, rep from * to end.
Row 3: Using yarn A K1, *using yarn B P1, using yarn A K1, rep from * to end.
Rows 4 and 5: As rows 2 and 3 **but** using yarn H instead of yarn B.
Rows 6 and 7: As rows 2 and 3 **but** using yarn G instead of yarn B.
Rows 8 and 9: As rows 2 and 3 **but** using yarn C instead of yarn B.
Rows 10 to 13: As rows 2 to 5.
Row 14: Using yarn A P1, *K1, P1, rep from * to end.
Change to 3¼mm (US 3) needles.
Beg and ending rows as indicated, using the **fairisle** technique as described on the information page and repeating the 54 row patt repeat throughout, cont in patt from chart, which is worked entirely in st st beg with a K row, as folls:
Cont straight until back meas 36 [37: 38: 38: 38] cm, ending with RS facing for next row.

Shape armholes
Keeping patt correct, cast off 6 [7: 8: 9: 10] sts at beg of next 2 rows. 117 [129: 143: 159: 177] sts.
Dec 1 st at each end of next 5 [7: 9: 11: 13] rows, then on foll 6 [7: 8: 10: 12] alt rows. 95 [101: 109: 117: 127] sts.
Cont straight until armhole meas 18 [19: 20: 21: 22] cm, ending with RS facing for next row.

Shape shoulders and back neck
Next row (RS): Cast off 5 [6: 7: 8: 9] sts, patt until there are

21 [23: 25: 28: 31] sts on right needle and turn, leaving rem sts on a holder.
Work each side of neck separately.
Dec 1 st at neck edge of next 4 rows **and at same time** cast off 5 [6: 7: 8: 9] sts at beg of 2nd row and 6 [6: 7: 8: 9] sts at beg of foll alt row.
Work 1 row.
Cast off rem 6 [7: 7: 8: 9] sts.
With RS facing, slip centre 43 [43: 45: 45: 47] sts onto a holder (for neckband), rejoin yarns and patt to end.
Complete to match first side, reversing shapings.

LEFT FRONT
Using 2¾mm (US 2) needles and yarn A cast on 64 [70: 78: 88: 98] sts.
Row 1 (RS): K1, *P1, K1, rep from * to last st, K1.
Joining in and breaking off colours as required, now work in striped 2 colour rib as folls:
Row 2 (WS): Using yarn A K1, P1, *using yarn B K1, using yarn A P1, rep from * to end.
Row 3: Using yarn A K1, *using yarn B P1, using yarn A K1, rep from * to last st, using yarn A K1.
Rows 4 and 5: As rows 2 and 3 **but** using yarn H instead of yarn B.
Rows 6 and 7: As rows 2 and 3 **but** using yarn G instead of yarn B.
Rows 8 and 9: As rows 2 and 3 **but** using yarn C instead of yarn B.
Rows 10 to 13: As rows 2 to 5.
Row 14: Using yarn A *K1, P1, rep from * to end, inc 0 [1: 1: 0: 0] st at end of row. 64 [71: 79: 88: 98] sts.
**Change to 3¼mm (US 3) needles.
Beg and ending rows as indicated, cont in patt from chart as folls:
Cont straight until left front matches back to beg of armhole shaping, ending with RS facing for next row.
Shape armhole
Keeping patt correct, cast off 6 [7: 8: 9: 10] sts at beg of next row. 58 [64: 71: 79: 88] sts.
Work 1 row.
Dec 1 st at armhole edge of next 5 [7: 9: 11: 13] rows, then on foll 6 [7: 8: 10: 12] alt rows. 47 [50: 54: 58: 63] sts.
Cont straight until 14 [14: 16: 16: 18] rows less have been worked than on back to beg of shoulder shaping, ending with RS facing for next row.
Shape front neck
Next row (RS): Patt 33 [36: 40: 44: 49] sts and turn, leaving rem 14 sts on a holder (for neckband).
Keeping patt correct, dec 1 st at neck edge of next 8 rows, then on foll 2 [2: 3: 3: 4] alt rows. 23 [26: 29: 31: 37] sts.
Work 1 row, ending with RS facing for next row.
Shape shoulder
Cast off 5 [6: 7: 8: 9] sts at beg of next and foll alt row, then 6 [6: 7: 8: 9] sts at beg of foll alt row **and at same time** dec 1 st at neck edge of 3rd row.
Work 1 row.
Cast off rem 6 [7: 7: 8: 9] sts.

RIGHT FRONT
Using 2¾mm (US 2) needles and yarn A cast on 64 [70: 78: 88: 98] sts.
Row 1 (RS): K2, *P1, K1, rep from * to end.
Joining in and breaking off colours as required, now work in striped 2 colour rib as folls:
Row 2 (WS): Using yarn A P1, *using yarn B K1, using yarn A P1, rep from * to last st, using yarn A K1.
Row 3: Using yarn A K2, *using yarn B P1, using yarn A K1, rep from * to end.
Rows 4 and 5: As rows 2 and 3 **but** using yarn H instead of yarn B.
Rows 6 and 7: As rows 2 and 3 **but** using yarn G instead of yarn B.
Rows 8 and 9: As rows 2 and 3 **but** using yarn C instead of yarn B.
Rows 10 to 13: As rows 2 to 5.
Row 14: Using yarn A (inc in first st) 0 [1: 1: 0: 0] time, P1 [0: 0: 1: 1], K1, *P1, K1, rep from * to end. 64 [71: 79: 88: 98] sts.
Complete to match left front from **, reversing all shapings and working first row of neck shaping as folls:
Shape front neck
Next row (RS): Using yarn A K14 and slip these sts onto a holder (for neckband), patt to end. 33 [36: 40: 44: 49] sts.

SLEEVES
Using 2¾mm (US 2) needles and yarn A cast on 53 [57: 59: 59: 61] sts.
Now work rib rows 1 to 14 as given for back.
Change to 3¼mm (US 3) needles.
Beg and ending rows as indicated and **beg with chart row 29**, cont in patt from chart as folls:
Inc 1 st at each end of 3rd and every foll 4th row to 77 [79: 83: 95: 103] sts, then on every foll 6th row until there are 95 [99: 103: 107: 111] sts, taking inc sts into patt.
Cont straight until sleeve meas approx 45 [46: 47: 47: 47] cm, ending after same chart row as on back to beg of armhole shaping and with RS facing for next row.
Shape top
Keeping patt correct, cast off 6 [7: 8: 9: 10] sts at beg of next 2 rows. 83 [85: 87: 89: 91] sts.
Dec 1 st at each end of next 5 rows, then on every foll alt row until 59 sts rem, then on foll 11 rows, ending with RS facing for next row. 37 sts.
Cast off 6 sts at beg of next 2 rows.
Cast off rem 25 sts.

MAKING UP
Press as described on the information page.
Join both shoulder seams using back stitch, or mattress stitch if preferred.
Neckband
With RS facing, using 2¾mm (US 2) needles and yarn A, slip 14 sts on right front holder onto right needle, rejoin yarn and pick up and knit 22 [22: 24: 24: 26] sts up right side of front neck, and 5 sts down right side of back neck, K across 43 [43: 45: 45: 47] sts on back holder, pick up and knit 5 sts up left side of back neck, and 22 [22: 24: 24: 26] sts down left side of front neck, then K across 14 sts on left front holder. 125 [125: 131: 131: 137] sts.
**Joining in and breaking off colours as required, now work in striped 2 colour rib as folls:
Row 1 (WS): Using yarn A K1, P1, *using yarn B K1, using yarn A P1, rep from * to last st, using yarn A K1.
Row 2: Using yarn A K2, *using yarn B P1, using yarn A K1, rep from * to last st, using yarn A K1.
Rows 3 and 4: As rows 1 and 2 **but** using yarn G instead of yarn B.
Row 5: Using yarn A K1, *P1, K1, rep from * to end.
Using yarn A, cast off in rib.
Button band
With RS facing, using 2¾mm (US 2) needles and yarn A, pick up and knit 153 [159: 163: 167: 167] sts evenly along entire left front opening edge, from top of neckband to cast-on edge.
Complete as given for neckband from **.
Buttonhole band
Work to match button band, picking up sts up right front opening edge and with the addition of 9 buttonholes worked in row 2 as folls:

KEY

☐ A. Raw

■ B. Wood

● C. Russet

○ D. Quince

◣ E. Eau de Nil

✕ F. Lime Flower

· G. Chestnut

▲ H. Dark Apple

Right front

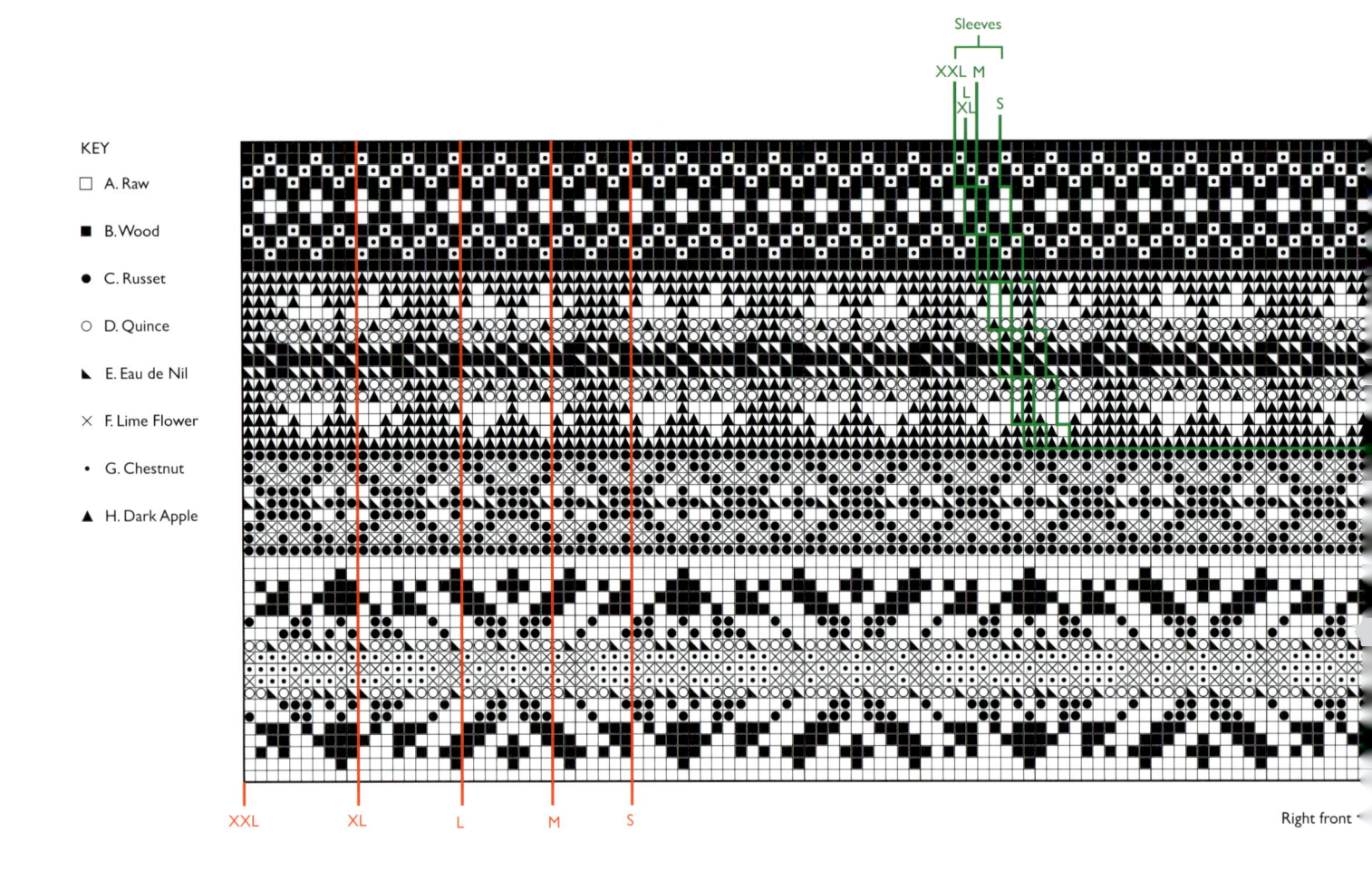

Row 2 (RS): Rib 4 [3: 5: 3: 3], *yrn, work 2 tog (to make a buttonhole), rib 16 [17: 17: 18: 18], rep from * 7 times more, yrn, work 2 tog (to make 9th buttonhole), rib 3 [2: 4: 2: 2].
Join side seams. Join sleeve seams. Insert sleeves into armholes.
Sew on buttons.
See information page for finishing instructions.

Sleeves
M XXL
L
S XL

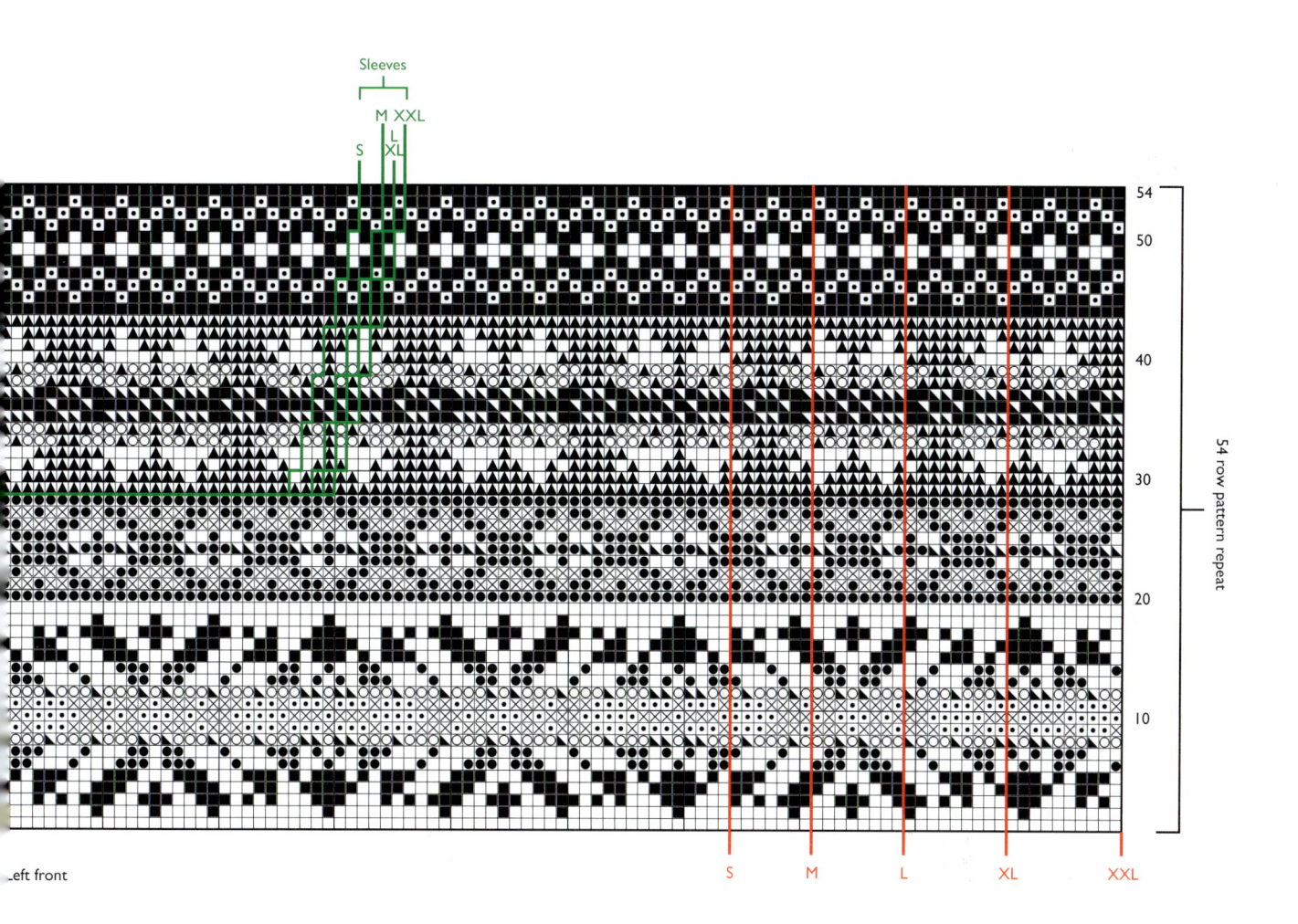

54
50
40
30
20
10

54 row pattern repeat

Left front

S M L XL XXL

93

WILD ROSE

● ● ●

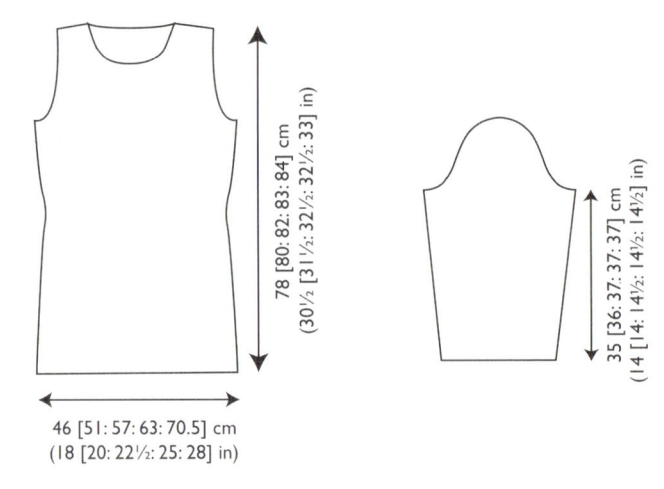

78 [80: 82: 83: 84] cm
(30½ [31½: 32½: 32½: 33] in)

46 [51: 57: 63: 70.5] cm
(18 [20: 22½: 25: 28] in)

35 [36: 37: 37: 37] cm
(14 [14: 14½: 14½: 14½] in)

	S	M	L	XL	XXL	
To fit bust	81-86	91-97	102-107	112-117	122-127	cm
	32-34	36-38	40-42	44-46	48-50	in

Marie Wallin British Breeds

A	Mulberry	3	4	4	5	5	x 25gm
B	Russet	2	3	3	3	3	x 25gm
C	Mallard	4	4	5	5	5	x 25gm
D	Rose	1	1	1	1	2	x 25gm
E	Lime Flower	2	3	3	3	3	x 25gm
F	Raw	2	3	3	3	3	x 25gm
G	Woad	2	2	3	3	3	x 25gm
H	Eau de Nil	2	2	2	2	2	x 25gm
I	Chestnut	1	1	1	1	1	x 25gm
J	Wood	3	4	4	4	5	x 25gm
K	Dark Apple	2	2	2	2	2	x 25gm
L	Quince	1	2	2	2	2	x 25gm

Needles
1 pair 2¾mm (no 12) (US 2) needles
1 pair 3¼mm (no 10) (US 3) needles

Tension
28 sts and 29 rows to 10 cm measured over patterned st st using 3¼mm (US 3) needles.

BACK
Using 2¾mm (US 2) needles and yarn F cast on 151 [165: 181: 199: 219] sts.

Row 1 (RS): K1, *P1, K1, rep from * to end.
Row 2: P1, *K1, P1, rep from * to end.
These 2 rows form single colour rib.
Join in yarn J.
Stranding yarn not in use across **WS** of work (this is front of work on WS rows, and back of work on RS rows), now work in 2 colour rib as folls:
Row 1 (RS): Using yarn F K1, *using yarn J P1, using yarn F K1, rep from * to end.
Row 2: Using yarn F P1, *using yarn J K1, using yarn F P1, rep from * to end.
Rep last 2 rows until work meas 4.5 cm, ending with RS facing for next row.
Break off yarn J and cont using yarn F **only**.
Rep rows 1 and 2 of single colour rib once more, ending with RS facing for next row.**
Change to 3¼mm (US 3) needles.
Beg and ending rows as indicated, using the **fairisle** technique as described on the information page and repeating the 80 row patt repeat throughout, cont in patt from chart, which is worked entirely in st st beg with a K row, as folls:
Work 8 [10: 12: 12: 12] rows, ending with RS facing for next row.
Keeping patt correct, dec 1 st at each end of next and 13 foll 6th rows. 123 [137: 153: 171: 191] sts.
Work 17 [17: 19: 19: 19] rows, ending with RS facing for next row.
Inc 1 st at each end of next and 2 foll 14th rows, taking inc sts into patt. 129 [143: 159: 177: 197] sts.
Work 15 rows, ending after chart row 68 [70: 74: 74: 74] and with

RS facing for next row. (Back should meas approx
56 [57: 58: 58: 58] cm.)
Shape armholes
Keeping patt correct, cast off 5 [6: 7: 8: 9] sts at beg of next 2 rows. 119 [131: 145: 161: 179] sts.
Dec 1 st at each end of next 5 [7: 9: 11: 13] rows, then on foll 4 [5: 6: 8: 10] alt rows. 101 [107: 115: 123: 133] sts.
Cont straight until armhole meas 20 [21: 22: 23: 24] cm, ending with RS facing for next row.
Shape shoulders and back neck
Next row (RS): Cast off 5 [5: 6: 7: 8] sts, patt until there are 19 [22: 24: 27: 30] sts on right needle and turn, leaving rem sts on a holder.
Work each side of neck separately.
Dec 1 st at neck edge of next 4 rows **and at same time** cast off 5 [6: 6: 7: 8] sts at beg of 2nd row, then 5 [6: 7: 8: 9] sts at beg of foll alt row.
Work 1 row.
Cast off rem 5 [6: 7: 8: 9] sts.
With RS facing, slip centre 53 [53: 55: 55: 57] sts onto a holder (for neckband), rejoin yarns and patt to end.
Complete to match first side, reversing shapings.

FRONT
Work as given for back until 18 [18: 20: 20: 22] rows less have been worked than on back to beg of shoulder shaping, ending with RS facing for next row.
Shape front neck
Next row (RS): Patt 33 [36: 40: 44: 49] sts and turn, leaving rem sts on a holder.
Keeping patt correct, dec 1 st at neck edge of next 8 rows, then on foll 4 [4: 5: 5: 6] alt rows. 21 [24: 27: 31: 35] sts.
Work 1 row, ending with RS facing for next row.
Shape shoulder
Cast off 5 [5: 6: 7: 8] sts at beg of next and foll 2 [0: 1: 1: 1] alt rows, then – [6: 7: 8: 9] sts at beg of foll – [2: 1: 1: 1] alt rows **and at same time** dec 1 st at neck edge of 3rd row.
Work 1 row.
Cast off rem 5 [6: 7: 8: 9] sts.
With RS facing, slip centre 35 sts onto a holder (for neckband), rejoin yarns and patt to end.
Complete to match first side, reversing shapings.

SLEEVES
Using 2¾mm (US 2) needles and yarn F cast on 67 [71: 73: 73: 75] sts.
Work from ** to ** as given for back.
Change to 3¼mm (US 3) needles.
Beg and ending rows as indicated, cont in patt from chart, **beg with chart row 61**, as folls:
Inc 1 st at each end of 3rd and every foll 4th row to 79 [81: 85: 97: 105] sts, then on every foll 6th row until there are 95 [99: 103: 107: 111] sts, taking inc sts into patt.
Cont straight until sleeve meas approx 35 [36: 37: 37: 37] cm, ending after same chart row as on back to beg of armhole shaping and with RS facing for next row.
Shape top
Keeping patt correct, cast off 5 [6: 7: 8: 9] sts at beg of next 2 rows. 85 [87: 89: 91: 93] sts.
Dec 1 st at each end of next 5 rows, then on every foll alt row until 57 sts rem, then on foll 13 rows, ending with RS facing for next row. 31 sts.
Cast off 5 sts at beg of next 2 rows.
Cast off rem 21 sts.

MAKING UP
Press as described on the information page.
Join right shoulder seam using back stitch, or mattress stitch if preferred.
Neckband
With RS facing, using 2¾mm (US 2) needles and yarn F, pick up and knit 24 [24: 26: 26: 28] sts down left side of front neck, K across 35 sts on front holder, pick up and knit 24 [24: 26: 26: 28] sts up right side of front neck, and 5 sts down right side of back neck, K across 53 [53: 55: 55: 57] sts on back holder dec 1 st at centre, then pick up and knit 5 sts up left side of back neck.
145 [145: 151: 151: 157] sts.
Row 1 (WS): P1, *K1, P1, rep from * to end.
Join in yarn J.
Row 2: Using yarn F K1, *using yarn J P1, using yarn F K1, rep from * to end.
Row 3: Using yarn F P1, *using yarn J K1, using yarn F P1, rep from * to end.
Rows 4 to 9: As rows 2 and 3, 3 times.
Using yarn F, cast off in rib.
Join left shoulder and neckband seam. Join side seams. Join sleeve seams. Insert sleeves into armholes.
See information page for finishing instructions.

KEY

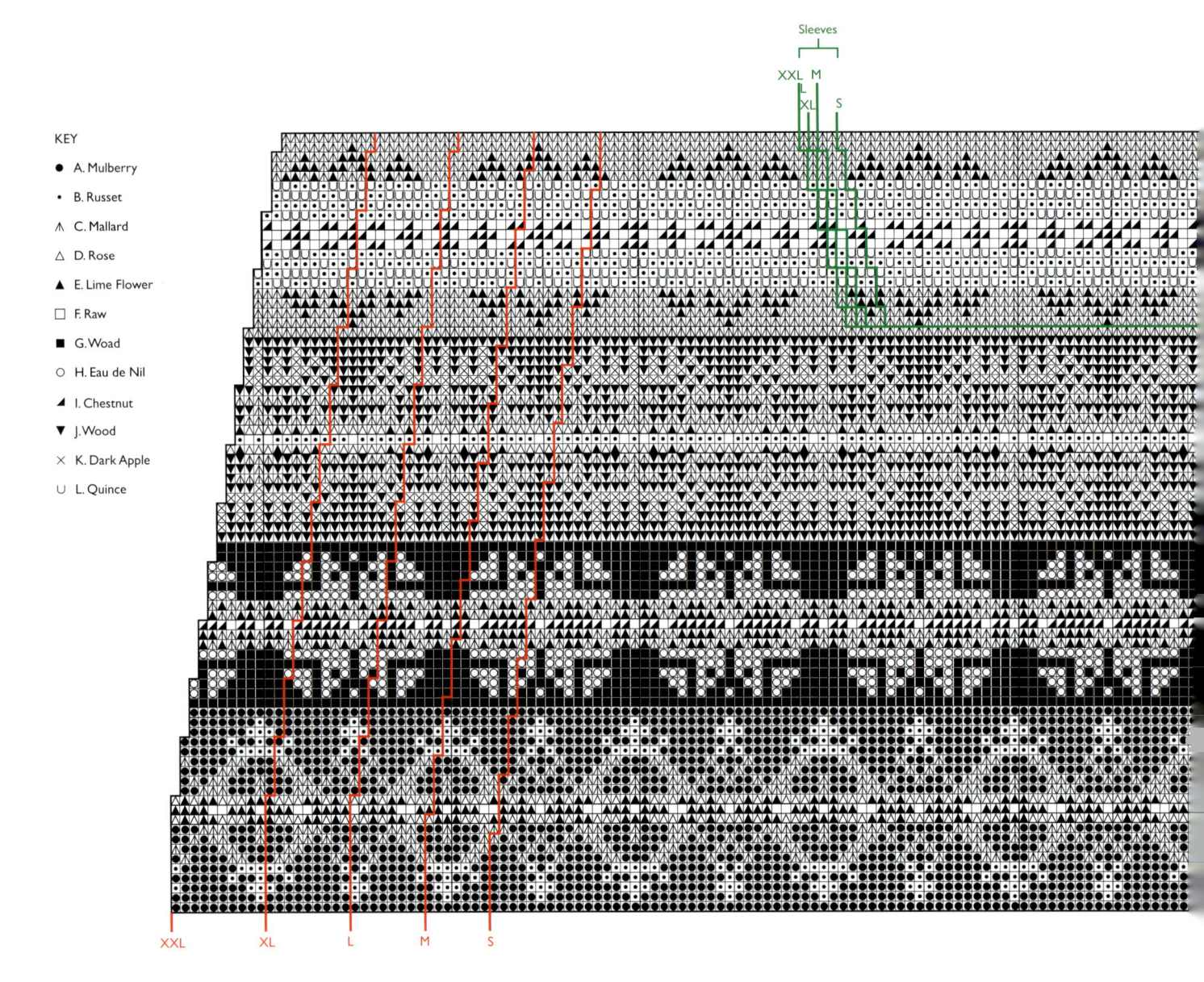

- ● A. Mulberry
- · B. Russet
- ∧ C. Mallard
- △ D. Rose
- ▲ E. Lime Flower
- □ F. Raw
- ■ G. Woad
- ○ H. Eau de Nil
- ◢ I. Chestnut
- ▼ J. Wood
- × K. Dark Apple
- ∪ L. Quince

Sleeves: XXL, L, XL, M, S

XXL, XL, L, M, S

Sleeves
M XXL
L
S XL

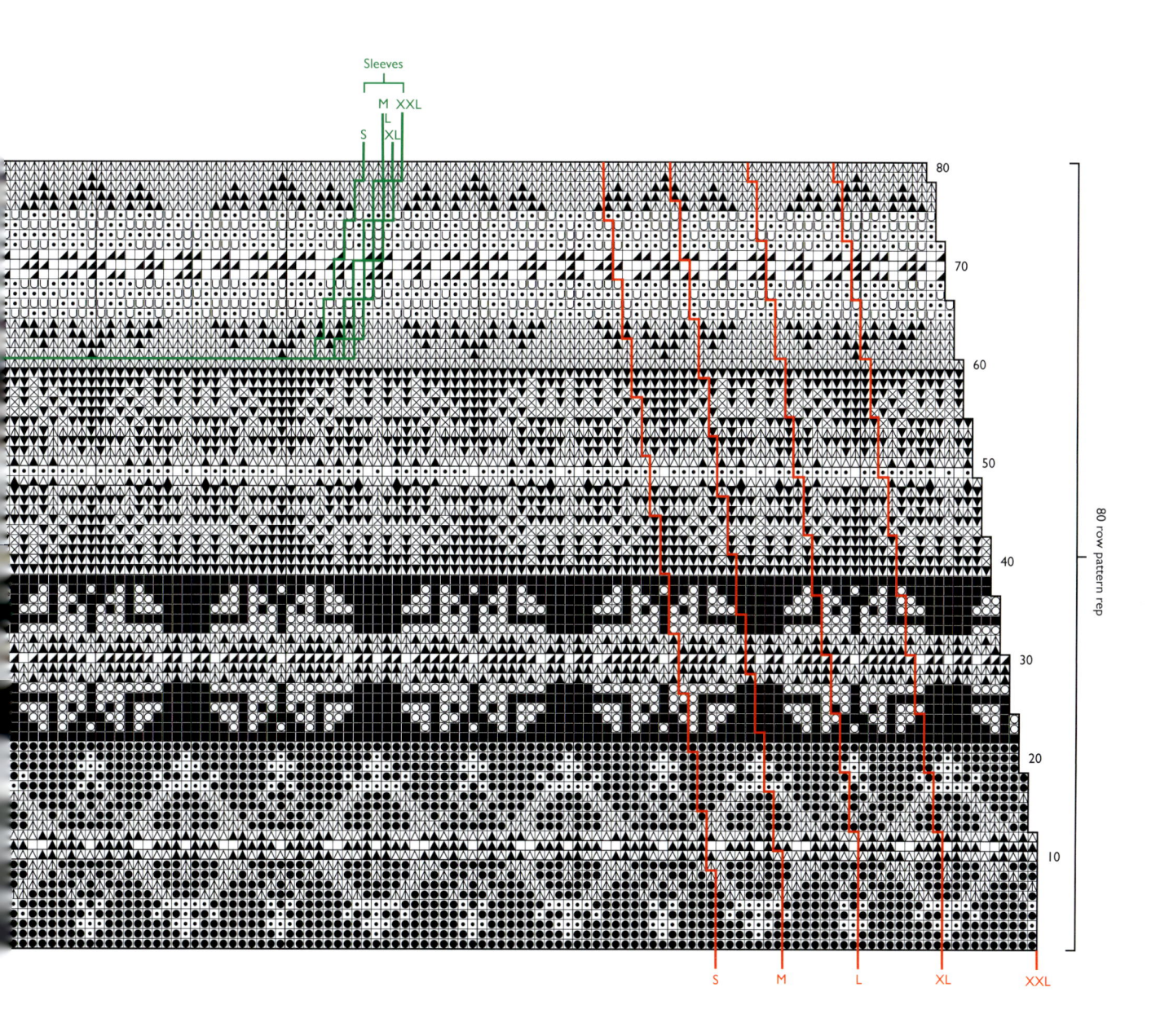

80 row pattern rep

S M L XL XXL

BEACON HILL COUNTRY PARK

….is one of my favourite places to walk with my husband and dogs. I have been visiting Beacon Hill for nearly twenty five years and over that time I have seen the park's natural heathland restored to its former beauty. However, it's the dense woodland that I love, the trees are truly majestic and quite magical.

Beacon Hill Country Park covers over 135 hectares of land comprising of woodland, heathland, grassland, wildflower meadows and adjoining farmland. At the summit of the hill at 248m, you are rewarded with panoramic views across Leicestershire.

The open heathland of Beacon Hill is of special interest, providing an important habitat for a wide variety of wide plants, animals and insects. Due to its ecological and geological importance, much of the park is designated a Site of Special Scientific Interest (SSSI).

To encourage the growth of heathland plants, the park now grazes English Longhorn and Highland Cattle as well as Manx Loaghtan and Hebridean sheep. It's great to see these animals at home in the landscape, as well as doing a good job helping restore the heathland, they add a certain drama to the park.

The rocks at the summit of Beacon Hill are amongst some of the oldest in the world, dated around 700 million years. The rocks originally developed on the sea bed in horizontal layers and over millions of years these were compressed and buckled into the dramatic shapes that you see today.

For more information:

Tel: 0116 305 5000
Email: countryparks@leics.gov.uk
Website: www.leicscountryparks.org.uk/beacon-visitor/

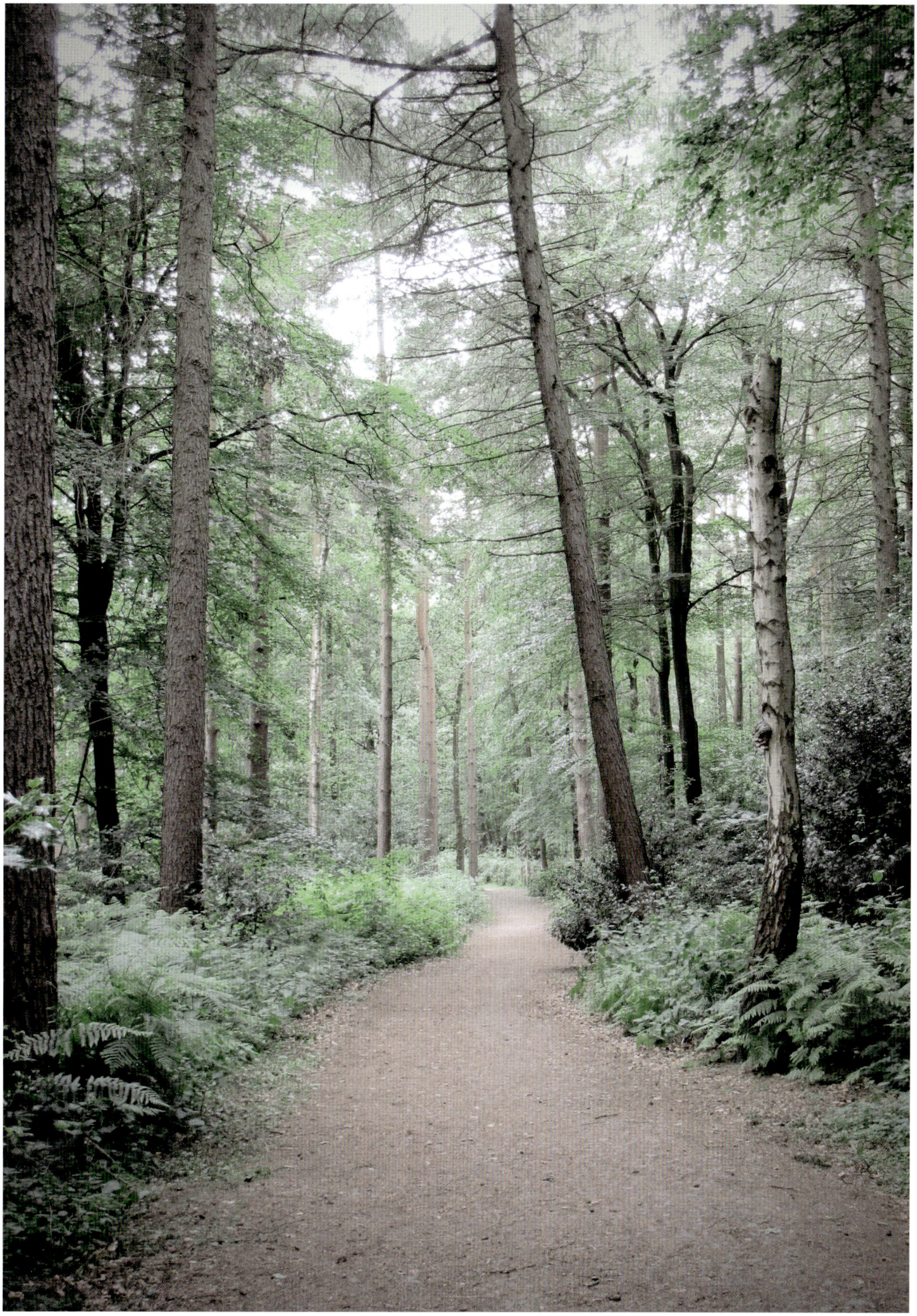

marie wallin
HANDKNIT & CROCHET

BRITISH BREEDS

A fine blend of wool, spun in Devon, from the Bluefaced Leicester, Exmoor, Wensleydale & Zwartbles sheep breeds.

www.mariewallin.com

BRITISH BREEDS

Over my thirty two year career in knitwear design, I have become passionate about natural fibres, British Wool in particular. Supporting our amazing British sheep breeds and our limited yarn spinning industry became important to me whilst working for Rowan and developing the 'Purelife' range of yarns.

Having now been an independent designer for over four years, it was a natural progression for me to create my own branded yarn and this had to be made from British Wool.

BRITISH BREEDS has taken two years to develop into the beautiful, soft, bouncy 4 ply yarn that it is today. Worsted spun in Devon by John Arbon and his wonderful team, BRITISH BREEDS is available initially in twelve lovely autumnal shades. It took a long time to finalise the colour palette as I had to be sure that all twelve colours work well together in Fair Isle knitting but also that each shade is a beautiful individual colour for single colour knitting.

BRITISH BREEDS is made from four different British sheep breeds: Bluefaced Leicester, Exmoor Horn, Wensleydale and Zwartbles. The wool fibre from each breed adds a certain characteristic to the yarn…

Bluefaced Leicester adds the beautiful softness, Exmoor Horn adds the softness too but this sheep produces a white fleece therefore adding a 'cleanness' to the blended tops making for more successful dyeing. Wensleydale adds the strength and lustre and Zwartbles adds the bounce or springiness.

To produce the yarn, the Bluefaced Leicester, Exmoor Horn and Wensleydale wool fibres are first blended together and then dyed into various coloured tops. These coloured tops are then blended together using a 'recipe' to create each of the twelve base colours. Each colour base is then blended with the undyed Zwartbles fibre creating the lovely mélange effect. Once the yarn is spun it is sent to Edward Hill's Ltd in Bradford to be steam relaxed and balled into 25g balls. The steam finishing 'opens up' the yarn creating the full, light appearance and handle. I decided to have BRITISH BREEDS balled instead of hanked as I wanted knitters to start knitting immediately without having the trouble to wind it beforehand.

I am very proud of the BRITISH BREEDS yarn and of the designs in WILDWOOD. I hope you enjoy knitting from this collection using my new yarn and that it becomes one of your favourite yarns to knit.

CHESTNUT	DARK APPLE	EAU DE NIL	LIME FLOWER
MALLARD	RUSSETT	QUINCE	RAW
ROSE	MULBERRY	WOAD	WOOD

WILDWOOD

STEEKING

Steeking is a traditional method of turning a sweater knitted in the round into a cardigan. This is done by knitting extra stitches and then edging these before cutting. The word 'steek' quite often fills the average knitter with dread at the thought of cutting knitting that has taken a long time to work. Once the initial fear has been conquered it is an easy and pleasurable technique to do. Steeking is most successful when the knitting yarn is 100% Wool as the 'sticky' fibres 'felt' together to help prevent any loose stitches from running. However, as my BRITISH BREEDS yarn is worsted spun and therefore softer, I am recommending that you do an extra reinforcement of your steek with a line of hand or machine stitching before picking up the stitches for the front bands on a cardigan or sleeves on an armhole.

Do not try and steek cotton yarns as the fibres are short and smooth and therefore are more difficult to work.

Note: the steek stitches are referred to in numbers 1 to 9, from right to left. The steek stitch ie. the one that is cut is steek stitch 5 and is in the centre of the group of nine stitches.

Below and on the next three pages I explain how to steek using two techniques, crochet reinforcement and stitch reinforcement.

CROCHET STEEKING

1. When wanting to steek a design, extra stitches need to be added at the centre front or armholes. Normally an odd number of stitches are added, I now add an extra nine stitches for my steeks. These nine stitches are then worked as a part of the Fair Isle pattern and are shown on the chart. You will notice that the chart has 5 steek stitches at the beginning of the round and 4 steek stitches at the end. Therefore the new round and the new colours are introduced on steek stitch 5, the first stitch on the chart. It is **very important that you do NOT weave any loose ends across the steek stitch (steek stitch 5)**, as this could cause the stitches to pull apart once cut. Generally I weave in the two new colours away from the steek as I knit the round from right to left. The two old colours I leave and sew in by hand from left to right after the knitting is complete. I have worked the steek stitches in a 'birdseye' pattern as it is on the chart for 'Hawthorn'. However, if you prefer, work the steek stitches in straight lines ie. dark colour over dark, light colour over light and so on.

2. With RS facing and starting at the welt edge and using a fine crochet hook (I use a 2.50mm (US B1/C2) hook for most steeks) work one chain stitch and start to work a double crochet (dc) (sc) into each stitch as follows: push the hook into the left hand leg of vertical steek stitch 4 and then into the right hand leg of vertical steek stitch 5 and complete a dc (sc) through both legs. Work a dc (sc) into each stitch all the way up the garment, work one ch. Break off the yarn.

3. With RS facing rejoin the yarn and work in the same way down the garment from top to bottom, working a dc (sc) into the left hand leg of vertical steek stitch 5 and the right hand leg of vertical steek stitch 6. Break off yarn.

4. Now spread out the fabric and you will see a vertical line of horizontal stitches have appeared where vertical steek stitch 5 was, this is the cutting line.

5. Carefully cut up this 'ladder' and the cut edges will disappear into the crochet 'edge' on either side of the fabric.

6. The fabric is now ready to be folded back to the WS of the garment. This can be held in place by hand stitching with the fold along the 1st and 9th vertical steek stitch. The back of the steek can then be covered if perferred with a pretty woven ribbon or knitted strapping. A steek worked in wool can be left uncovered as this will felt as the garment is washed and worn. Cardigan trims or sleeves can now be worked by picking up and knitting the stitches along the first and last vertical pattern stitches immediately before and after the nine stitch steek section.

Generally I find that crochet steeking with 100% Wool is quite secure and I would normally not work a line of stitching by hand or machine but if you are new to this method then I would recommend that you work a line of stitching by hand or machine along steek stitches 3 and 7 **BEFORE** picking up stitches for front bands or sleeves.

CROCHET STEEKING

1.

2.

3.

4.

5.

6.

Pick up stitches along this vertcial line

Steek stitches
9 8 7 6

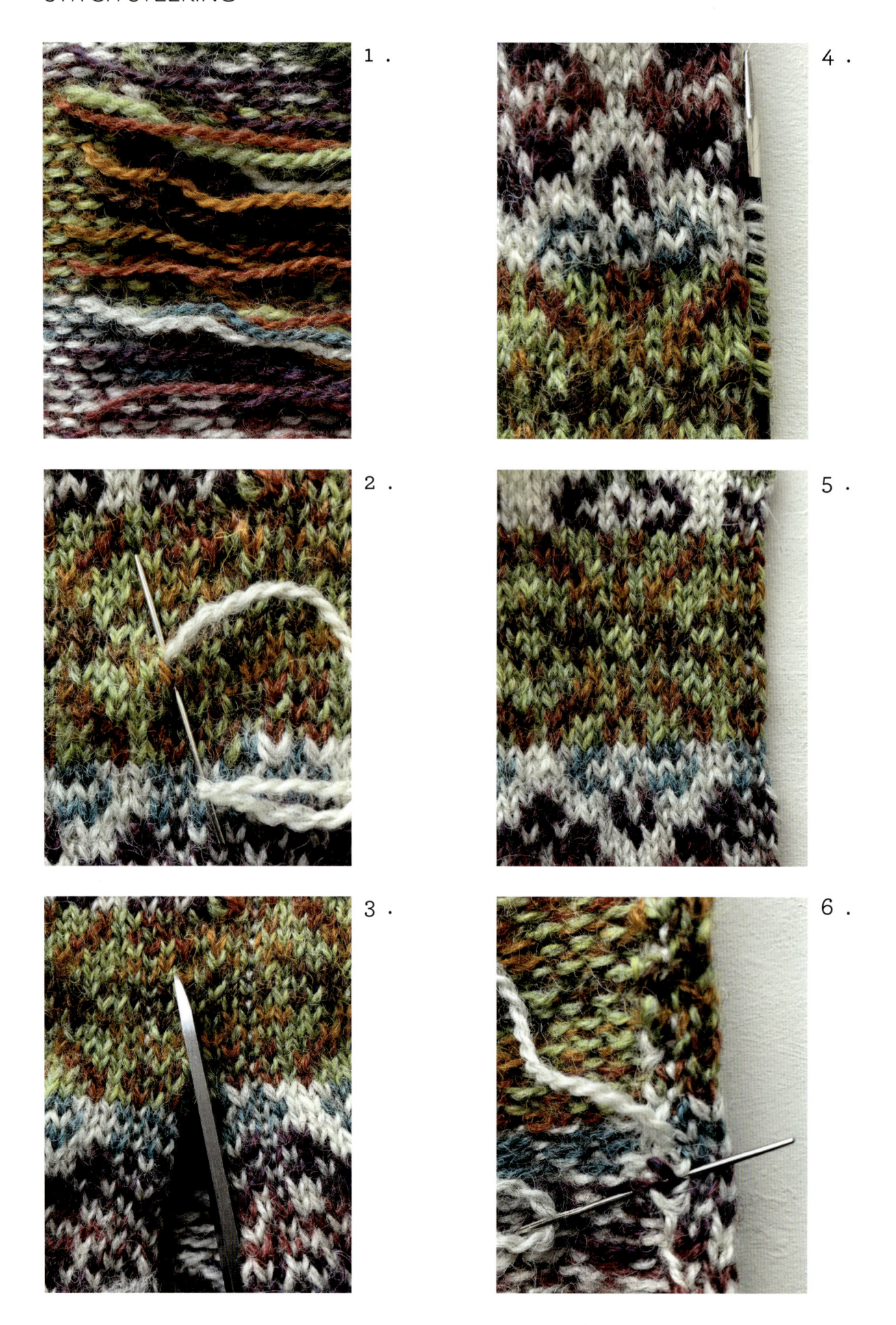

STITCH STEEKING

1.

2.

3.

4.

5.

6.

7.

STITCH STEEKING

If you do not like to crochet or you feel this method is too slow or difficult then try steeking by stitch reinforcement. The steek stitches are knitted in exactly the same way as described for the CROCHET method but leave the ends unwoven.

1. DO NOT WEAVE or SEW in the loose ends as these will be trimmed off later.

2. Machine stitch or hand stitch using back stitch a double line up the centre of vertical steek stitches 2 and 8.

3. Cut up the centre of steek stitch 5.

4. Pick up the stitches for the front bands or sleeves and work these as according to the pattern. **The image shows the stitches being picked up in one go, I prefer to pick up one stitch at a time and knit it.**

5. Trim the steek edges to steek stitch 3 and 7. Please note: the image shows the fabric WITHOUT the trim. It is important that the stitches for the front bands or sleeves are picked up BEFORE the steek is trimmed back.

6. Fold the steek edges back to WS and stitch in place by over sewing in one direction up the work and back down the work in the opposite way creating a cross stitch appearance.

7. This image shows the appearance of the finished steek from the RS without the trims added.

Finally, whichever method you choose you will soon realise that steeking is not difficult or scary at all! Be brave!

INFORMATION

TENSION
Achieving the correct tension is one of the most important factors when knitting one of my designs. I cannot stress highly enough that you really do need to knit a tension square BEFORE you start to knit the garment. The tension stated on each of my patterns must be achieved to ensure that the garment fits correctly and that it matches the measurements stated on the size diagram. I recommend that you knit a square using the number of stitches and rows stated on the pattern tension plus 3 or 4 stitches and rows. To check your tension, place the knitted square on a flat surface and mark out a 10cm square using pins as markers. Count the number of stitches and rows between the pins. If you have too many stitches, then your knitting is too tight, knit another square using a thicker needle. If you have too few stitches, then your knitting is too loose, knit another square using a thinner needle. It is also important to keep checking your tension whilst you are knitting your garment especially if you are returning to knit after leaving your work for a period of time.

SIZING
The patterns are written giving the instructions for the smallest size, for the other sizes work the figures in the brackets. The measurements stated on the size diagrams are the measurements of your finished garment AFTER pressing.

MODEL SIZE
Georgia is 5'8" tall and is a standard size 8/10 and she is wearing the smallest size in each photograph.

FAIR ISLE - STRANDED COLOUR WORK
Fair Isle is one of the main methods of adding colour into knitting. Fair Isle is used when two colours are to be worked repeatedly along a row. The colour not being used is stranded fairly loosely behind the stitches being worked. It is very important not to pull this stranded yarn too tight as this will pucker your knitting and your stitch tension will be too tight, make sure to spread your stitches to ensure that they remain elastic. I would recommend that you carry the stranded or floating yarn over no more than 5 stitches when using a DK or 4 Ply yarn, and no more than 3 stitches when using an Aran or Chunky yarn. Weave the stranded colour under and over the colour being worked if you have to knit a colour over more than the recommended amount.

FINISHING
Finishing your garment beautifully is another important factor when making one of my designs. Good finishing will ensure that your garment fits correctly and washes and wears well. I urge you to spend time pressing and stitching your garment together, after all you've just spent a lot money and time knitting it using lovely yarns and the last thing you want to do is ruin it with bad finishing!

PRESSING
Firstly sew in any loose ends to the wrong side of the knitting. Block out each piece of knitting and then gently steam press on the WS on the knitting using a WARM steam iron. To do this, make sure that you hover the iron over the knitting and smooth flat with your hand. DO NOT put the full weight of the iron on the knitting even over a damp cloth as this will flatten it too much. Always press using a WARM iron on the wrong side of the knitting over a protective cloth (this can be damp or dry) and have the steam setting switched on the iron. Pay particular attention to the sides or edges of each piece as this will make the sewing up both easier and neater. Take special care with the welts and cuffs of the knitting – if the garment is fitted then gently steam the ribs so that they fill out but remain elastic. If the garment is a boxy, straight shape then steam press out the ribs to correct width.

STITCHING
When stitching the pieces together, remember to match areas of colour, texture or pattern very carefully where they meet. I recommend that you use mattress stitch wherever possible, this stitch gives the neatest finish ensuring that the seam lays flat.

Having knitted your pieces according to the pattern instructions, generally the shoulder seams of the front and back are now joined together using mattress stitch. Work the neck trim according to the pattern instructions and then join the neckband seams using mattress stitch if required. Knit neck bands or collars to the length stated in the pattern instructions, slightly stretching the trims before measuring if knitted in garter stitch or horizontal ribbing. Please take extra care when stitching the edgings and collars around the neck of the garment as these control the stretch of the neck. The sleeves are now normally added to the garment, take care to match the centre of the sleeve head to the shoulder seam. Ideally stretch the sleeve head into the armhole and stitch in place, if the sleeve head is too large for the armhole then check your tension as your knitting may be too loose. Join the underarm and side seams. Slip stitch any pockets or pocket lining into place and sew on buttons corresponding to the button holes lining up the outside edge of the button with the edging join or seam.

Carefully press your finished garment again to the measurements stated on the size diagram.

DIGITAL CHARTS
If you wish to receive a PDF copy of the charts within this collection then please send an email to: info@mariewallin.com with your request.

AFTERCARE
Ensure that you wash and dry your garment according to the care instructions stated on the BRITISH BREEDS ball bands. If your

garment uses more than one type of yarn then wash according to the most delicate. Reshape your garment when slightly damp and then carefully press to size again.

BUTTONS
The buttons used in this collection were kindly supplied by Textile Garden:

Textile Garden
1 Highland Croft
Steyning
BN44 3RF
UK
Tel: +44 (0) 1903 815759
     +44 (0) 7736 904109
Email: sales@textilegarden.com
Web: www.textilegarden.com

EXPERIENCE RATING
For guidance only.

● suitable for a beginner knitter with a little experience.

●● suitable for a knitter with average ability.

●●● suitable for the experienced knitter

KNITTING ABBREVIATIONS

K	knit
P	purl
st(s)	stitch(es)
inc	increas(e)(ing)
dec	decreas(e)(ing)
st st	stocking stitch (1 row K, 1 row P)
g st	garter stitch (K every row)
beg	begin(ning)
foll	following
rem	remain(ing)
rev st st	reverse stocking stitch (1 row K, 1 row P)
rep	repeat
alt	alternate
cont	continue
patt	pattern
tog	together
mm	millimetres
cm	centimetres
in(s)	inch(es)
RS	right side
WS	wrong side
sl 1	slip one stitch
psso	pass slip stitch over
p2sso	pass 2 slipped stitches over
tbl	through back of loop
M1	make one stitch by picking up the horizontal loop before the next stitch and knitting into the back of it
M1P	make one stitch by picking up the horizontal loop before the next stitch and purling into the back of it
yfwd	yarn forward
yrn	yarn round needle
meas	measures
0	no stitches, times or rows
-	no stitches, times or rows for that size
yon	yarn over needle
yfrn	yarn forward round needle
wyib	with yarn at back

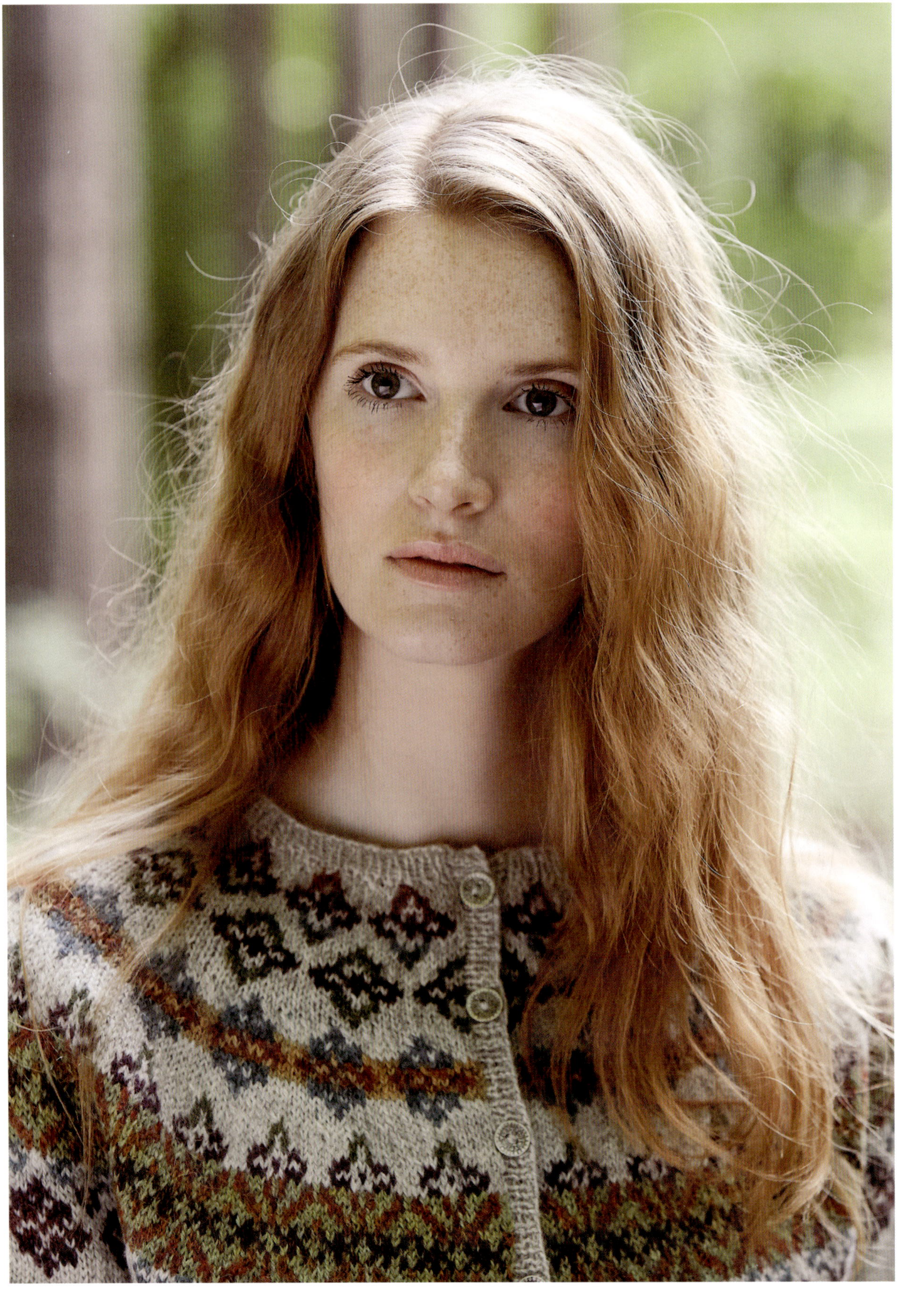